D0629067

DELAWARE DIARY

DELAWARE DIARY
EPISODES ✦ IN ✦ THE ✦ LIFE ✦ OF ✦ A ✦ RIVER

Frank Dale

Rutgers University Press
New Brunswick, New Jersey

Third paperback printing, 2002

Library of Congress Cataloging-in-Publication Data

Dale, Frank
    Delaware diary : episodes in the life of a river / Frank Dale.
        p.   cm.
    Includes bibliographical references (p.   ) and index.
    ISBN 0–8135–2282–x (cloth : alk. paper).—ISBN 0–8135–2283–8
    (pbk. : alk. paper)
        1. Delaware River (N.Y.–Del. and N.J.)—History.   2. Delaware River
    Valley (N.Y.–Del. and N.J.)—History.   I. Title.
    F157.D4D28   1996
    974.9—dc20   95–39440
                                                                         CIP

British Cataloging-in-Publication information available

Copyright © 1996 by Frank T. Dale
All rights reserved
No part of this book may be reproduced or utilized in any form or by any
means, electronic or mechanical, or by any information storage and retrieval
system, without written permission from the publisher. Please contact Rutgers University Press, Livingston Campus, Bldg. 4161, P.O. Box 5062, New
Brunswick, New Jersey 08903. The only exception to this prohibition is
"fair use" as defined by U.S. copyright law.
Manufactured in the United States of America

To Diana
Best Friend, Lover, Wife

CONTENTS

PREFACE AND ACKNOWLEDGMENTS

I was quite young the first time I saw the river; it was probably in 1928. My family lived in North Jersey, but my grandparents lived in eastern Pennsylvania—at Nicholson to be exact, site of the famous Tunkhannock Viaduct. We made frequent trips to Pennsylvania to visit these grandparents, as well as assorted aunts, uncles, and cousins. (Later on, we visited the cemetery where they were buried.) We always crossed the river at Columbia on the stout, old covered bridge that had survived all of the floods up to that time. (The bridge was finally done in by a hurricane named Diane in 1955, in the worst natural calamity that the valley has ever seen.) We'd cross over in that dark, narrow, creaking wooden tunnel and come out the other side in Pennsy, at Portland. Thus, I received my first geography lesson—Pennsylvania and New Jersey are separated by the Delaware River.

We'd drive along the river on the twisting, narrow road toward the village of Delaware Water Gap, but we'd always stop along the way at one of the many gingerbread and buttermilk stands. My mother loved the buttermilk, and we kids needed the fresh air, car sickness being a nearly genetic disorder among the Dale children. These places always had a deer in a pen for us kids to look at; a much rarer sight then than now. After this break, we'd proceed into the village, past the fine hotels and the crowded streets, then into Stroudsburg, Scranton, and finally past the huge concrete viaduct into Nicholson. In those days it was a long trip.

The Delaware River was the first river I ever saw, and it is still my favorite. A few years ago, after a seven-month vagabond journey in a VW van—I'd outgrown car sickness by this time—my wife Diana and I came home to New Jersey on Interstate 80 through the Water Gap. It was October and the leaves were in full color. We were greeted by the most breathtakingly beautiful sight of the entire trip, and we'd seen the Rockies, Yellowstone, even the Grand Canyon. Nothing matched *this* sight.

What saved the upper Delaware from industrial destruction is that it is not much good as a commercial stream. This book goes into some detail about early entrepreneurs who attempted to turn the river into a Hudson or a Mississippi, but could never quite pull it off. It's too shallow in spots, too filled with rifts and rapids, and its water level is apt to get even lower in the dry months. The only commercial ventures along the upper river that are prospering today are the canoe liveries. The Delaware is great for canoeing; it offers stretches for paddling that vary in difficulty, so that anyone from novice to expert can have a good time on its waters. There's always enough river for everyone to do his own thing—canoeing, fishing, swimming. A local nudist canoe club makes regular trips downriver almost unnoticed.

The river is cleaner than it used to be. When we were making those visits to Nicholson years ago, the shad got no farther upriver than Philadelphia because of the pollution. A whole generation of residents and visitors had never seen shad or striped bass on the up-per river, or a bald eagle flying overhead. But the shad, striped bass, and bald eagle are all there now, and the water is so clean you can drink it without hesitation—at least I do. Forests cover hillsides that a century ago had been scalped bald. Much of the Delaware has be-come in fact what it was proclaimed to be in a bill signed by Presi-dent Jimmy Carter on November 10, 1978: a wild and scenic river.

I've attempted to relate events in the life of this exciting river. I hope you enjoy them. Of course, your pleasure will be enhanced by getting out on the river, or walking along its shore and observing some of the reminders of a bygone era. Canoe through or simply walk beside Foul Rift or Skinners Falls, and you'll understand why timber sailors cursed these obstacles two hundred years ago. If you choose to canoe through Foul Rift, you can look to the Pennsylvania side and see iron rings put in the cliffs there by Robert Hoops; these rings were used by crews on Durham boats to help pull themselves upriver through the fierce current. Hoops's good friend, George Washington, was president when the work was done.

On some especially bitter Christmas Day, take the kids to Washington Crossing State Park on the Pennsylvania side. There you can watch a reenactment of Washington's recrossing of the river on his way to attack Trenton, one of the most significant military operations in the history of the United States. Fort Delaware is still there on Pea Patch Island in the bay, and in the summer a launch will take you out to the island. The fort was saved and restored by a group of history buffs who call themselves the Fort Delaware Society.

Upstream, you can still cross the river on a bridge at Columbia. The piers of the old covered bridge are still there, but they support a footbridge now. Or go farther upstream to Lackawaxen and canoe down toward Barryville, New York. Launch in front of the Zane Grey Museum on the Pennsylvania shore and, down in the water, you'll see part of the old wooden dam that gave the raftsmen fits. Almost immediately you'll pass under John Roebling's aqueduct, built to carry canal boats over the river safe from onrushing rafts. Here, too, you can look up at a hill on the New York side where the Iroquois under Joseph Brant slaughtered some forty militia soldiers. The rock shelter where Surgeon Tunsten died with his wounded is still there.

By most measurements, many of the episodes in this book happened "just yesterday." Actual participants of some of the more recent events were interviewed whenever possible. Several of the canoeists in the 1933 marathon are still around, for example. Of the "river rats," Rita Back (now Rita Back Norton) is as spunky as ever and lives today at the river's edge. Howard Cooley still seems young and lives within a stone's throw of the river at Frenchtown, and the Kleedorfer brothers are still sharp. Survivors of the flood of 1955 abound, and veterans of the Tocks Island War are as outspoken, tough, and inspired as ever; just talk to Casey Kays, Dick Harpster, or Nancy Shukaitis. Much of this history is still alive and ongoing; it doesn't end.

I received a lot of help from a lot of people in writing this book. I'd like to mention them and I will, even with the possibility, nay, probability, of overlooking someone.

I used all the local libraries: Warren County, Hackettstown, Morris County, Sussex County, Hunterdon County, Washington, Philadelphia, Newark, and Port Jervis, and made extensive use of their microfilmed newspapers—local, regional, and national—as well as other materials. I got from all the librarians a smile and the help I needed. I wish I knew all their names so I could thank them individually. Especially helpful to me was Easton Library's Marx Room, with its collections of local history and unpublished manuscripts. The people that work there, Barbara Bauer and Sandra Froberg, know everything—or at least where to find what they don't. The *Easton Express-Times* and Carol King, the paper's librarian, arranged for several of the photos of the flood of 1955. I used the East Stroudsburg University library for information on the Tocks Island Dam and the squatters. The folks at both the paper and the university went out of their way for me and guided me to some unexpected information.

Historical societies provided invaluable help, giving me the benefit of some very detailed expertise and, at a reasonable price, copies of photos from their archives. Mike Knies of the Canal Museum in Easton was one of these. Peter Osborne and the Minisink Valley Historical Society have a highly professional operation, and Peter gave me help above and beyond the call of duty. Temple University's Urban Archives were a source of some great photos of the canoe marathon, and I thank George Brightbill for digging them up for me. Sarah Sullivan and Ed Sheehy of the Philadelphia Maritime Museum gave me some last-minute assistance. I spent a couple of days at the Fort Delaware Society's archives in Delaware City, Delaware, and Martha Bennett was most generous, tolerant, and helpful. On the same trip I went farther south to Lewes, formerly Whorekill, and visited Delaware State's Zwaanendael Museum; there I was helped by Beth Gott and Adele Hudson. Mary Curtis, a cultural resources specialist on the Upper Delaware for the National Park Service, revealed a deep knowledge of timber rafting, which she shared most generously. Her ancestor, Charles T. Curtis, was a raftsman of great renown on the river, so she came by it naturally.

Mary Murrin of the New Jersey Historical Commission offered much good advice. I also received from the commission a small grant that helped me research the Tocks Island piece. Mary never gave me all I asked for in the way of grant money, but in turning me down she was always very considerate of my fragile ego. She's a fine person. Dale Berger with the New Jersey Division of Forests and Parks provided information on Manunka Chunk Island, which now belongs to the state.

There is a whole other category of historians—amateurs, I guess you'd call them—who made this book possible. Most of them have fine personal collections of photographs and many have bits of information that just aren't available elsewhere. These people are not paid professionals, have acquired their photo collections at considerable personal expense, and in many cases are authors in their own right. Nevertheless, they shared everything they had with me, without hesitation and without charge. I never had any of them turn me down. On the contrary, they went out of their way to help. They are: Betty Jo King, Ron Wynkoop Sr., Bill Dopke, Dick Harpster, Jim Lee, Bill Lifer, Neil Brodt, Carl Baxter, and Richard Ransom. Their only motivation must have been friendship, and I am truly honored. Thank you.

And a final word for a couple of old-timers who aren't around anymore but who got me going in the right direction many years ago: Thanks, Bob and Bill.

DELAWARE DIARY

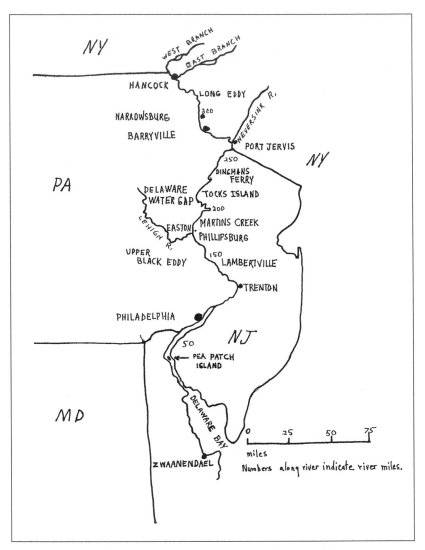

The Delaware River. (Map courtesy of Diana Dale)

INTRODUCTION

This book is a collection of episodes in the life of the Delaware River and its valley, beginning with the coming of European explorers and settlers. By way of "setting the stage," however, let me say a few words about the original residents, the Lenni-Lenape.

Ten thousand to twenty thousand years ago, much of the earth's water was in the form of continental glaciers. Undoubtedly, the first-comers to North America simply walked on dry land from Asia, crossing what is now the Bering Strait between Siberia and Alaska. Most archaeologists feel that ancestors of the Lenni-Lenape arrived in one of these waves of migration, thousands of years before the arrival of the first Europeans.

Giovanni da Verrazano saw them first when he arrived off the shores of North America in 1524. It was love at first sight. He wrote his French sponsor, Francis I:

> These people are the most beautiful and have the most civil customs that we have found on this voyage. They are taller than we are; they are a bronze color. . . . the hair is long and black and they take great pains to decorate it; the eyes are black and alert, and their manner is of the ancients. . . . they have all the proportions belonging to any well-built men. Their women are just as shapely and beautiful.

When the Dutch arrived in the Delaware Bay a hundred years later, there were probably twelve thousand Lenni-Lenape living in New Jersey, eastern Pennsylvania, lower New York State, and northern Delaware, an area known as Lenapehoking. Those who were living in the lower Delaware Valley came to be called Delawares. Those who settled farther up the valley in the vicinity of Minisink Island and Sussex County were called Minsi or Munsee.

The Lenni-Lenape were farmers, growing corn, beans, squash, pumpkins, and a little tobacco in small plots. They also hunted wild game, fished, and gathered berries and nuts from the forests. They lived in semi-permanent villages of related people with kinship traced through the mother's family. Their homes were either round wigwams or longhouses built of a sapling framework covered with bark or brush.

Most of their villages were on or near the Delaware or its tributaries, and much of their activity centered around the river. According to archaeological evidence, the Lenni-Lenape or their ancestors constructed dugout canoes as far back as the Archaic Period, six thousand years ago. They would locate and fell a tree of appropriate size, using a controlled fire around the trunk, then flatten one side and build a fire on it. Charred portions were gouged or scraped out, and new fires set until the interior of the log became sufficiently hollow. The exterior was shaped, the ends pointed, and a handsome river-worthy craft produced. This same technique was followed even after the Europeans arrived, except that some metal tools were then used. The Lenni-Lenape rarely built bark canoes due to the lack of the large birch trees found farther north.

The Delaware and its major tributaries provided abundant food for the Lenni-Lenape. In the spring—a time of physical and social renewal after the lean and isolating winter months—herring, alewife, sturgeon, shad, and eel made their way upriver to spawn by the billions, and from their canoes the Lenni-Lenape speared these fish and tended their traps or weirs in the river. The fish were so abundant that they could be caught with a bare hand; those not eaten were dried for later use. Lenni-Lenape living along the lower river or the bay hunted whales, seals, and porpoises. These mammals had to surface to breath, and when they did they would be harpooned and then finished off by spear or arrow. In addition, the Lenni-Lenape killed migrating birds by the thousands, and some groups traveled to the Jersey shore to gather shellfish and hunt sea birds.

Archaeological evidence also indicates that groups of Lenni-Lenape traded among themselves. Pottery, flint, and foodstuffs were traded, or exchanged for wampum. When the Europeans arrived, the Lenni-Lenape paddled canoes loaded with beaver and other hides to Dutch or Swedish outposts along the river.

Relationships between the Lenni-Lenape and the Europeans were tolerable as long as they were temporary. European crews needing water, fuel, or food might come ashore and get these things from the local inhabitants by exchanging cloth, tools, brass kettles, and jewelry. Fur traders collected beaver and other pelts from the Lenni-Lenape in exchange for axes, kettles, cloth, liquor, and rifles. The goods changed hands and the traders sailed away without incident. Unfortunately, the intolerance of the Lenni-Lenape for liquor would soon have a debilitating effect on their society. (The British tried prohibiting liquor trade with the Lenni-Lenape, but, like other prohibitions in United States history, it didn't succeed.) Also, the Lenni-Lenape came to prefer European weapons to hunt game, thus becoming dependent on the traders for shot and powder—and for the repair of the cheaply made trade weapons. When beaver in the Delaware Valley were trapped to extinction, the Lenni-Lenape, now dependent on European goods, were more willing to trade away their land.

When the Europeans settled permanently near the Lenni-Lenape, the frequent contact aggravated cultural differences. The Dutch, whose New Netherland at one time comprised most of present-day Connecticut, New York, New Jersey, and Delaware, seemed especially prone to conflict with their new neighbors. They were staunch Calvinists who considered all non-Christians to be pagans, children of the devil. They attempted to convert the Lenni-Lenape but had little success. In 1628 a Dutch man-of-God in New Netherland, Pastor Jonas Michaelius, expressed a commonly held opinion: "I find them entirely savage and wild, strangers to all decency, yea, uncivil

and stupid as garden poles, proficient in all wickedness and godless-
ness; devilish men who serve nobody but the devil." With such strong
feelings extant, violence was sure to follow.

Chapter 1 cites the execution, by order of the governor of Zwaanendael, of a Lenni-Lenape chief for stealing, and the retaliatory massacre of the entire settlement by the tribe. Just six years later, in 1637,
the governor of New Netherland, Willem Kieft, sent a force across
the Hudson River at night to attack a friendly group of Lenni-Lenape
encamped at Pavonia, near present-day Jersey City, "to make them
wipe their chops." A Dutch eyewitness wrote after the attack:

> The soldiers returned to the fort having murdered
> eighty Indians, and considered they had done a deed
> of Roman valor in murdering so many in their
> sleep. . . . Infants were torn from their mother's
> breasts and hacked to pieces in the presence of the
> parents, others were cut, struck, and pierced. Some
> were thrown in the river to drown. Some escaped
> with their hands or legs cut off.

Thirty more Lenni-Lenape were massacred on Corlaers Hook on
Manhattan the same night and several were beheaded, their heads
brought back as trophies—all this to let the Lenni-Lenape know
"who was boss."

A Lenni-Lenape group called the Hackensacks sought revenge for
this undeserved brutality. In 1643 and again in 1655, the settlements
of some five hundred Dutch were attacked and burned on the Jersey
side of the Hudson, and many farmers were killed. This episode in
Dutch colonial history is referred to as Governor Kieft's War.

The Swedes in the Delaware Valley welcomed the Lenni-Lenape
as long as they could supply beaver pelts, but when this valuable
commodity began to run out, their attitude changed. Governor Johan
Printz in 1644 said of the Lenni-Lenape: "Nothing would be better
than that a couple of hundred soldiers should be sent here and kept
here until we broke the necks of all of them in the river." Word of this
attitude spread rapidly to all the Lenni-Lenape clans in the east.

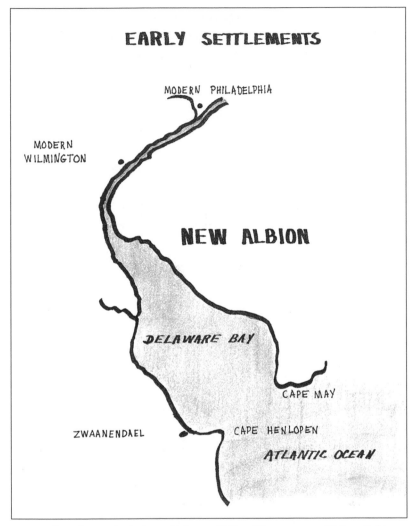

Early settlements in the lower Delaware Valley. (Map courtesy of Diana Dale)

The English, when they occupied New Netherland and the Delaware Valley in 1664, were less aggressive toward the Lenni-Lenape than the Dutch and Swedes had been. Indeed, Quaker William Penn was known among the Native Americans for his fairness and generosity. Nevertheless, the English were as determined as the Dutch to expand their land holdings, and deeds were drawn up in the legalese of the day. The Lenni-Lenape could hardly read any of the paperwork to which they affixed their "marks," and they probably didn't understand the concept of private ownership of land. Often these land agreements were facilitated by the application of generous amounts of rum.

One of the most notorious land scams perpetrated against the Lenni-Lenape was the infamous Walking Purchase of 1737. Two sons of William Penn, John and Thomas, definitely were not "chips off the old block"—ethically, at least. They had acquired a deed signed by their father with the Lenni-Lenape, they said, that gave to William and his heirs a generally triangular piece of land in the Pocono Mountains area of eastern Pennsylvania. One boundary was to be the Delaware River; another boundary would be a line generally north-west into the forest "as far as a man could walk in a day and a half." The third line would be drawn at a right angle from the end of the walked line back to the river. The Lenni-Lenape commonly used this walking measurement; to them it meant a leisurely stroll with plenty of breaks for rest, food, and smoking. They anticipated that the day-and-a-half walk through heavy forest would cover no more than thirty-five miles. However, prior to the walk, the Penns hired men to cut a path almost double that distance through the dense growth. They then engaged three of the fastest men in the area and offered each a prize of five hundred acres of land if they were successful.

The walk started early in the morning of September 19. A team of Lenni-Lenape went along to supervise but could not keep up with the almost jogging pace. Of the three men hired to make the trip, two collapsed from exhaustion. Only one man, Edward Marshall, finished after a run of sixty-five miles. This hoax gained for the Penn brothers twelve hundred square miles of prime hunting land in northeastern Pennsylvania. It also earned the undying hatred of the Lenni-Lenape, who in revenge killed Marshall's pregnant wife and, in another raid, his son, Peter. Marshall went into hiding on an island in the Dela-ware that today bears his name. Other settlements in the Walking Purchase territory were attacked, especially in Smithfield Township

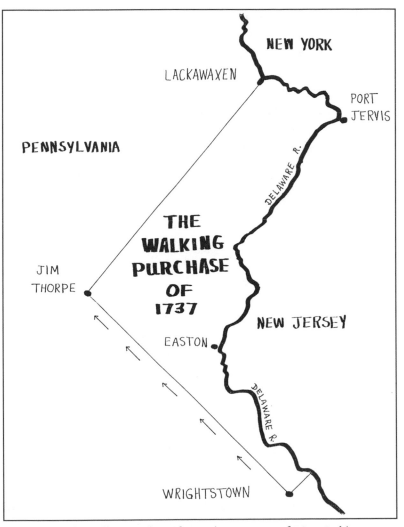

The Walking Purchase of 1737. (Map courtesy of Diana Dale)

and at Depuis and Brodheads in the Water Gap area. Lenni-Lenape war parties even struck across the river in New Jersey, killing members of the Swarthout and Cole families. For a time the territory remained virtually deserted. The Moravians at Nazareth sheltered hundreds of refugees from these attacks.

By the mid-1700s, the Lenni-Lenape civilization in the Delaware Valley was in sharp decline. The tribe's population had started to decrease with the arrival of the first Europeans, and it had never reversed itself. Warfare, alcohol abuse, and disease had taken their toll. Frequent epidemics of smallpox, malaria, scarlet fever, measles, and syphilis had devastated the Lenni-Lenape, who had no immunity against these European scourges. But the loss of their lands to the white farmer and timbercutter was the primary agent of the tribe's decline and disbursal. Conferences between the settlers and the Lenni-Lenape at Crosswicks, New Jersey, and Easton, Pennsylvania, resulted in yet more land lost.

As early as 1758, the Brotherton Indian Reservation was created at Indian Mills in South Jersey. Run by missionaries, it attracted mostly Native Americans who had converted to Christianity. By the end of the century, however, it ceased to exist.

A trickle of Lenni-Lenape migrants had started westward when the first Europeans arrived in the Delaware Valley. They first located in the Susquehanna Valley, then moved on to the valley of the Allegheny River. Eviction as a result of the Walking Purchase accelerated this relocation, and European movement into Pennsylvania pushed the Lenni-Lenape farther westward. Treaties were made, then broken. Some of the Lenni-Lenape, mostly Munsees, moved out of the United States altogether and settled in Ontario, Canada. Many Delawares moved on to Ohio and Indiana, finally settling in Oklahoma, Kansas, and Wisconsin.

A few Lenni-Lenape still live in the Midwest; others remain in Ontario. These few ancestors of our valley's early inhabitants have been subdued, assimilated, converted, and diluted; they are far removed from the once-proud inhabitants of the beautiful land called Lenapehoking. Giovanni da Verrazano would hardly recognize them.

I

Nasty
Little
Village

he names of the first European visitors to Delaware Bay are familiar to every schoolchild. Giovanni Verrazano arrived in 1524; Henry Hudson, in 1609. Hudson, sailing for the Dutch East India Company, wrote in the ship's log about the strong current in the bay, indicating that the bay was fed by a river, but shoals discouraged further exploration. Neither captain felt that this was the much-sought-after water route to India, and Hudson would ultimately become more intrigued by the mighty river that today bears his name.

One year after Hudson's arrival, an Englishman, Captain Samuel Argall, entered the bay in his ship, the *Discovery*. He named the body of water after Lord De La Warr, the new lord governor and captain-general of the nearby Jamestown colony. De La Warr never saw his namesake bay and Argall never returned to it. Neither knew that a river flowed into it.

The Dutch, the leading traders of the day, were the first to move into the Delaware Valley. Basing their claim on Hudson's brief stopover, they enjoyed almost exclusive fur trading, whaling, and fishing activity in the bay and river for more than half a century. The Swedes arrived later in limited number, but the Dutch seemed to tolerate this minor incursion. In 1616 Dutch captain Cornelis Hendrickson explored the river as far north as the juncture of the Schuylkill, near modern Philadelphia, in a boat small enough to maneuver among the shoals and sandbars. By 1631 the Dutch had established a base in the river on Burlington Island and had built a trading post called Fort Nassau across the river from Philadelphia. They had also purchased from the local Lenni-Lenape and founded a whaling station on Cape Henlopen at the entrance to South Bay, as they called it. The Dutch named this last settlement Zwaanendael, meaning "Valley of Swans." It was built on an arm of land between the bay and a fine oyster-filled stream that they named Hoornkill, after their home village in Netherland.

Whales, probably the giant finback, wintered by the hundreds in the lower bay, and sailors would occasionally see them farther upriver cavorting in fresh water. The Dutch, who operated a very successful whaling station in Greenland, had been quick to see a profitable opportunity; whale oil, like beaver pelts, was much in demand in Europe. In addition to whaling equipment, the Zwaanendael settlers brought with them cattle, seeds, and plows. They built houses— some were constructed of yellow brick that came over as ship's ballast—and a palisade for protection.

These first colonizers, thirty men, were brought to Zwaanendael by Captain Peter Heyes on the *De Walvis*. They arrived too late in the season for the whales but just in time for spring planting. When Heyes and the *De Walvis* departed, the crops were in and the cows were calving; all seemed well. But when Captain Peter DeVries arrived the following December to help with the whaling, he found the palisade and many of the houses destroyed and the fields strewn with the bones of the unfortunate settlers. Of those left there the previous spring, only one, Theunis Willemsen, survived. The Lenni-Lenape had struck, it was learned later, because the colony's governor had had a chief beheaded for stealing. DeVries, in his journal, writes of this earliest colonization effort in the New World as having been "sealed with the bloud of a great many sowles."

Little was heard from the settlement for the next several years, and historians have conjectured that it was abandoned after the attack. We now know that it was used as a trading post. In 1658 the Dutch reestablished the village, again buying the land from the Lenni-Lenape. This time they built a fort.

In July 1663 Peter Cornelis Plockhoy, a German Moravian, arrived at the settlement with forty-two followers. These hard-working zealots envisioned a socialistic community based on the equality of man and founded on Christian principles. Plockhoy later moved to Germantown, Pennsylvania, but many of his followers remained at the settlement or in the surrounding area. They became the backbone of the revived village. The mixture of nationalities now living in the village resulted in a change in name; Zwaanendael was dropped and the village became known as Hoornkill.

The following year bad things began to happen again to the colony, as the English decided to oust the Dutch from their holdings. The Duke of York, brother to England's King Charles II, captured New Amsterdam, then forced the surrender of the Dutch in New Jersey. Hoornkill was claimed by Lord Baltimore's nearby colony, Maryland; indeed, the settlement was within Maryland's territory, but the greedy Duke of York ignored the claim and Hoornkill was caught in the middle. The duke's forces, under Sir Robert Carr, attacked the village and other Dutch settlements on the bay. The soldiers were permitted to pillage and keep all they could carry; Carr enriched himself by confiscating the choicest land and stealing a new commodity in the colony, slaves. The Dutch, however, by taking the oath of allegiance to the King of England, were allowed to stay and to keep their homes and farms.

Hoornkill then became Hoerekill, which, on the arrival of the English, was anglicized into Whorekill. In 1669 Baltimore decided to occupy this land on Delaware Bay. He created Worcester County, which included Whorekill, and offered land at low rents to attract settlers. Newcomers from New Jersey, Virginia, and Pennsylvania were quick to move in. In June 1672 Baltimore commissioned Thomas Jones of Worcester to be captain of military forces in the area. Jones raided Whorekill to enforce loyalty to Lord Baltimore and threatened to kill the magistrate if he did not swear allegiance. Then England declared war on the Netherlands, and Baltimore and York set aside their differences to face the common enemy.

In 1673 the Dutch recaptured their New World holdings. Several Dutch navy vessels sailed to the Delaware and occupied posts around the bay, including Whorekill. The unfortunate citizens of the little village who just the year before had sworn allegiance to the King of England and then to Lord Baltimore, now, under the gun again, pledged loyalty to the new Dutch regime. Then the Dutch withdrew.

Governor Calvert of Maryland, Baltimore's son, now commissioned Captain Thomas Howell to raise a cavalry force and make a punitive attack on the village. Howell's troopers, heavily armed, thundered into Whorekill to teach the "fickle" burghers a lesson. They broke into houses, killed cattle, and terrified the citizens, who with alacrity swore allegiance to Calvert. Howell briefly occupied the "nasty little village," as he called it, but departed when he found it too poor to support his troops.

Howell and his band soon returned, apparently under new orders. Howell called on all the males in the village to report to him with their weapons and ammunition; he intended to conduct a military drill, he said. When everyone gathered, the soldiers disarmed them and Howell announced his real mission: he was going to burn every building in the village and would start in fifteen minutes. As the village went up in flames, some of the townspeople had to be restrained from attempting to rescue possessions and food. When the conflagration ended, one barn, partially destroyed, was all that stood. Howell left it as shelter for the pregnant women and babies, then carried away all firearms and boats. The victims now lacked transportation or security from attack, and the nearest settlement, New Castle, lay sixty miles away. Howell and his troops were treated as heros by Calvert and amply rewarded with the currency of the realm, tobacco.

Some of the villagers managed to reach New Castle but many were lost, killed by Lenni-Lenape or the freezing weather. A handful stayed behind in the barn that winter, and were eventually supplied with food and clothing by a rescue party from New Castle. So the little village "sealed in bloud" didn't die.

Under English rule, the port at the mouth of the bay began to prosper. Although the whaling industry faded, the port workers busily transshipped grain, timber, furs, and fish. The English officials laid out village streets, surveyed plots, and encouraged settlement. Soon the good citizens of Whorekill petitioned the authorities for a courthouse, a jail—and a name change. Governor Edmund Andros complied with all these requests, apparently selecting in 1682 a name that would reflect the improved status of the village: New Deal.

In the meantime the war with the Dutch ended, and again the lower Delaware Valley was fought over by the two rivals, York and Calvert. It took that great conciliator, William Penn, to bring order out of the chaos of conflicting claims and boundaries. Penn had received a grant from Charles II of a large province north of and bordering land claimed by both York and Calvert. However, he wanted to verify the borders of his province and have all competitive claims settled before he took title. First he convinced York to disqualify his claims to the west bank of the river and land along the bay. Penn accomplished this apparently impossible task easily, for York had fallen into disfavor with his brother, the king, and had been banished to Scotland. He could no longer look to the king to support his false title.

To conciliate Calvert's claim to the west bank, Penn disproved the Maryland governor's assertion that he had arrived there before any other Christian nation. Penn proved that the Dutch settlement at Whorekill predated the 1632 Maryland grant to Lord Baltimore, Calvert's father. With this victory, the three counties of Kent, New Castle, and Sussex became lower Pennsylvania. Under the governship of William Penn, New Deal became Lewestown, and then simply Lewes.

Lewes continued to grow, and its renown as the first sheltered port at the mouth of the river brought additional prosperity—and trouble. Lewes became a favorite port of call—and target—for pirates. Names such as Blackbeard, Avery, and Kidd became household words in the little village, and the depredations of these captains and their crews here and at towns along the coast continued until 1698. Early governors attempted reform and gave pardons on promises of good behavior, but all to no avail. It took pacifist William Penn to crack down hard on these seagoing bandits with punishment instead of pardons, thus finally defeating them.

In 1704 the counties of Kent, New Castle, and Sussex were taken from Pennsylvania and established as a colony of the Crown. As Philadelphia and Wilmington grew into major upriver cities, the need for skilled pilots to take ships through the shoaly river water also grew. A colony of these skilled pilots lived in Lewes and, hence, most ships destined for the cities had to make port there to pick up a pilot. Ships entering Delaware Bay also had to be ready for storms; Cape Henlopen could be as dangerous as Cape Hatteras in severe weather. (The salvage of these wrecks became a major source of income for sea captains living in the area.) A lighthouse built in 1765 served ships in the bay for 160 years, but wrecks occurred never-theless. (Years later, during a gale in 1889, forty-three vessels ran aground on Lewes beaches. In that same gale the pilot boat *Enoch Turley,* with five pilots and five seamen aboard, was swept out to sea and never seen again.) In 1776 the colonists adopted a constitution for the "Delaware State." During the Revolutionary War Delaware coastal towns suffered from raids and blockades by the British navy. On December 7, 1787, Delaware became the first state to ratify the Constitution of the new United States.

It all had begun with that much-abused settlement called Whore-kill, which survived because of the remarkable tenacity of its people. After statehood the only act of aggression against the village took place during the War of 1812. On April 5, 1813, a British naval squad-ron of 240 guns anchored offshore to blockade the bay and isolate the upriver cities. British Commodore J. P. Beresford sent a message to the people of Lewes that they must supply him with water and food—though His Majesty's government would be glad to pay, of course. The town officials refused any supplies and called in Colonel Sam Davis with about five hundred militia and a few artillery pieces.

The British fleet opened fire from afar—they were intimidated by Davis's cannon—and the bombardment lasted twenty-two hours. Davis's artillery ran out of shot, but local men and boys crawled out among the marsh grass and dunes and picked up incoming British shot of the same caliber. Eight hundred shells were fired by the British during the day-and-night barrage, with total casualties consisting of a dog, a hen, and a milk can—and one house that received a ball and is today a tourist attraction. When no white flag was raised in surrender, the British squadron sailed away without its supplies. The "nasty little village" had done it again.

2

LORD EDMUND PLOWDEN— ROYAL LOSER

n the beginning the English showed only a passing interest in Delaware Bay and its river. It's true that Captain Samuel Argall named the bay after the new governor of the Jamestown colony, Lord De La Warr, but Argall never explored beyond the bay or even saw the river. Other English ships visited—Thomas Dermer in 1620 and Thomas Yong in 1634—both looking for a northwest passage to the Pacific, but, unsuccessful at this, they departed the area. By this time, the Dutch were well established along the lower river and bay. During this period, the only English attempt at colonization in this area was the ill-fated venture by Sir Edmund Plowden.

An unhappy man, Sir Edmund was one of those unfortunate souls who wants to be liked but whose temperament attracts only dislike. In addition, he was totally inept in money matters. A Catholic, he served under that most Catholic of English monarchs, Charles I, who had a similar personality problem. Both men were dreamers whose dreams, in the end, turned to nightmares.

Plowden dreamed of a colony in the New World, a place where he could start his failed life anew. The place would not be large; rather, a nice neat square, 120 miles on each side, on the eastern bank of the Delaware River in what would become New Jersey. These dimensions would include most of the modern state as well as several islands in the river. Sir Edmund, when he petitioned the king for the grant, said he planned an initial settlement of five hundred people, much larger than any other English or Dutch settlement in the New World, and it would be devoted to the "making of wine, salt, and iron, fishing of sturgeon and mullet, and for cattle and corn for the colony, and for the . . . building of ships." The colony would bear the poetic name of New Albion. Neither he nor his monarch seemed to be concerned that Dutch Fort Nassau was located within the boundaries of New Albion, nor that most of the land belonged to the Lenni-Lenape.

Charles gave the grant as a reward for good services, but the financially strapped monarch demanded money as well. Fortunately, Plowden had married an heiress, Mabel Marriner, who, in the early years of the marriage at least, was willing to provide the needed cash. The charter gave Sir Edmund the territory as his exclusive possession. He could make and enforce laws, build fortifications, and make war. "The Right Honourable and Mighty Lord Edmund, by Divine Providence, Lord Proprietor, Earl Palatine, Governor and Captain-General of the Province of New Albion" received his charter on June 21, 1634.

Eight years passed before Sir Edmund departed for the New World, a difficult time for the colonizer. During this period his marriage failed and his wife demanded her money back. One respected historian reveals that Plowden and his wife, in what must have been happier times, had produced no less than eighteen offspring. Collecting funds for payment to his ex-wife, supporting this brood, and attempting to gather money for ships and supplies was a difficult, almost impossible, task. Businessmen who had invested in the project hadn't expected to wait eight years for a return on their investment and took Plowden to court. The harried lord, facing lawsuits and an angry wife, finally sailed for New Albion in August 1642.

Lack of funds and lack of faith in Plowden kept the expedition smaller than expected. For settlers, he could gather only some indentured servants and a few relatives, a far cry from his original grandiose scheme. He sailed to the Virginia colony at Jamestown, where he expected to pick up a pilot who could guide him to his holdings along the Delaware. Unfortunately, Sir Edmund had no reserve funds and had to borrow money to house and feed his expedition while in Virginia. And the pilot, not surprisingly, wanted his money in advance. Weeks dragged into months and the indentured servants began to desert him. Because Plowden could not pay the debts he incurred in Virginia, he was again plagued by lawsuits. At last, in May 1643, Plowden sailed for his beloved New Albion with what was left of his expedition, which now numbered only sixteen. Along the way those sixteen mutinied, put Plowden ashore on Smith's Island in Chesapeake Bay, then sailed off, leaving their hapless leader with neither food nor drink on an island whose only other inhabitants were wolves and bears. The mutineers reached Delaware Bay, where they found a Swedish outpost and asked to be put aboard the next ship to England. They nearly got away with their deed, until one of the female members of the group broke down and confessed. In the meantime Sir Edmund had been picked up from the island by a passing English vessel. He was hungry, dehydrated, and badly sunburned, but, fortunately, untasted by either wolves or bears. He sailed back to Jamestown and, when the mutineers returned there, had the ringleaders shot.

The destitute Lord of New Albion remained in Virginia for the next five years, running a store to support himself and trying to raise funds for another expedition. He sold passes to ships sailing for the Delaware River, his right under his charter, but the Swedish authorities along the Delaware refused to honor them and sent the ships back. Angry shipmasters demanded a refund and sued for the costs of a wasted trip. Again the luckless lord sank into financial trouble.

While Plowden kept store in Jamestown, the Dutch and Swedes were confronting each other over land along the Delaware, and two British colonies, Maryland and New Haven, were claiming ownership of land included in the grant for New Albion. It seemed to

Sir Edmund that his rights would come to naught in this turmoil. Then in 1649 his mentor, King Charles I, was deposed and beheaded, and grants made by the king came under a cloud.

It is unlikely that Sir Edmund ever saw New Albion. He returned to England, stopping at Boston and Manhattan along the way. When he reached England another Catholic king, Charles II (son of Charles I) occupied the throne, but things were no better for Sir Edmund. Records show he served two sentences in debtors' prisons and faced innumerable lawsuits during the final years of his sad life. "The Right Honourable and Mighty Lord Edmund" died a pauper in 1659.

On March 12, 1664, Charles II granted his brother the Duke of York (later to become James II) proprietary rights to most of the Dutch territory of New Netherland, including the capital at Manhattan and all of the land on the eastern side of the Delaware. This grant totally ignored Charles I's grant creating New Albion, bought and paid for by Sir Edmund and now the property of his sons.

In August 1665, Dutch governor Peter Stuyvesant, under threat of attack, surrendered to the British and New Amsterdam became New York. The Duke of York now controlled most of the Delaware Valley, including ill-fated New Albion.

In 1773 Sir Edmund's great-great-grandson, Francis Plowden, petitioned King George III to have his rights restored and to be able to collect rents from all those living on what should be his property in New Jersey. The petition was pigeonholed during the Revolutionary War, and after the war, of course, the land became the property of another nation. Undaunted, Francis published a pamphlet offering lands for sale in "his" New Albion, and in 1784 he hired attorney Charles Varlo to present his case to the American government and people. His aim was not to recover any land but to collect rents on the property, a tidy sum considering that New Albion included the whole State of New Jersey. Varlo met with George Washington, soon to become the first president of the new republic, and showed him voluminous documents to prove ownership, all to no avail.

It is not surprising that Washington still mistrusted the government of George III and looked with a jaundiced eye at anything coming from his recent enemy. And the good people of New Jersey had never heard of New Albion or Edmund Plowden, and they looked upon Varlo and Francis Plowden as harmless eccentrics.

But there is no doubt that the Plowdens' charter is as legitimate as William Penn's or Lord Baltimore's. In granting New Albion to the Duke of York, Charles II illegally confiscated land and violated property rights, something still sacred under English common law. We may not have heard the last of New Albion.

3

TIMBER RAFTS
ON THE RIVER

he earliest settlers along the upper Delaware found the river a poor transportation artery. The rapids, rifts, and falls that make this area a delight for modern canoeists were a deterrent to commercial river traffic. Local Lenni-Lenape preferred land trails to the fierce waters of the stream, and the Dutch, who mined copper on the banks of the river, carried their ore overland to the Hudson rather than risk it on the hazardous and uncertain Delaware.

Foul Rift, located one mile below Belvidere, blocked downriver passage except in times of high water until Major Robert Hoops of Belvidere, along with a crew of about twenty-five men, opened the channel in 1791. Hoops, who operated a business in Belvidere, was already something of a hero for getting food through to Washington's starving troops at Morristown during the hard winter of 1779–1780. Now he and his crew, under constant threat of attack from Lenni-Lenape, worked from August to October and cleared a channel through the rift using explosives and hand-held drills. At the same time, a passage through Wells Falls at New Hope was opened by another contractor. So effective were these improvements that the waterfront village of Belvidere built a large stone wharf into the river to handle the increased Durham boat traffic. Travel time to Philadelphia was cut by half.

Even with these improvements, several generations of die-hard nautical entrepreneurs remained frustrated in their attempts to conquer the river with sail or steam power. The only commercial craft ever to overcome the upper river and its hazards were the Durham boats, made famous by Washington's crossing of the Delaware above Trenton, and the timber rafts, which dominated river traffic during the nineteenth century.

The success of timber rafting, which started in the 1760s, was due in part to the breed of people who manned the rafts. These hardy mountain men on the upper reaches of the river had the requisite nerves of steel; the profits awaiting them at the Philadelphia shipyards provided the motivation. As part of the British Empire, the colonies operated under a system called mercantilism; they sold raw materials to England, then bought back manufactured goods. Because England set the prices and forbade the colonies to trade with foreign countries, the system became a hateful one to the colonists. In the early days of settlement, however, this system provided those who worked along the river with a ready market for their timber and with a rare source of cash income. In the colonial period, Philadelphia ranked second only to London in the value of its exports and imports.

Building and maintaining the British navy and merchant fleet, the largest in the world in the eighteenth century, was a herculean task. These wooden ships were constantly being consumed by war, storm, or worm. This last, a wood-boring gourmand, destroyed as many ships as the other two combined. Fabled English forests were depleted to meet the insatiable needs of the admiralty, and New World woodlands, especially those nearest the eastern seacoast, were soon called on to meet the demand. Thus timber rafting got its impetus.

Daniel Skinner, a Catskill Mountain man from Callicoon, New York, was the first to try this method. An ex-sailor, he saw the value of the tall pines, and in the spring of 1764 he threw a few "sticks" in the river and followed them downstream in a canoe. He made it to the naval shipyards at Philadelphia, but most of his logs remained on the banks of the Delaware. On his next attempt, he fastened some logs together to make a raft, mounted a long steering oar aft, put two men aboard as crew, and tried again. One man fell overboard and drowned, but Skinner and the surviving crew member, Josiah Parks, successfully rode their eighty-foot raft over Foul Rift and Trenton Falls to Philadelphia, where they were greeted as heroes. Pleased British shipbuilders dubbed Skinner "Lord High Admiral of the Delaware" and named Parks "Chief Bosun." For a while Skinner and Parks enjoyed a virtual monopoly on timber traffic, exacting a fee, payable in whiskey, from other raftsmen and even from their own crew. But the demand for timber was so great that Skinner and Parks lost control of the river trade.

The demand continued after the Revolution, although this time it came from the shipbuilders of the new nation. New Jersey and Pennsylvania forests furnished maple and oak for the ships' hulls; the forests of the Catskills supplied pine and hemlock for spars and masts. One especially fine specimen from these forests became a mast for a forty-four-gun frigate, the U.S.S. *Constitution,* built in the Philadelphia yards for the fledgling United States Navy. This mast carried its ship's sails through battles with Barbary pirates at Tripoli and in several engagements against the British fleet during the War of 1812; through it all, the *Constitution* went without a defeat. Because of the ship's indestructibility, the crew nicknamed it "Old Ironsides."

For 1828, *Hazard's Register of Pennsylvania* reported that one thousand rafts containing fifty million feet of lumber descended the Delaware during the rafting season. These numbers increased each year for the next fifty years. All winter, timber cutters felled trees as close to the river as possible to get ready for spring. The logs accumulated on the ice at an eddy. When spring thaw dropped them into the water, they were pinned together into rafts thirty to forty feet wide and up to two hundred feet long, and steering oars were mounted fore and aft to each. The steersman, aptly called the *ironman,* was responsible for guiding the bulky craft through the turbulent and rocky river. Rafts moved only in high water or *freshet,* which always occurred in the early spring and sometimes in the fall. Raftsmen who

Large raft on the river at Matamoras, Pennsylvania. (Photo courtesy of the Minisink Valley Historical Society, Port Jervis, New York)

started downriver too early in the spring were apt to run into ice jams, a situation that could result in the destruction of the raft or at least its abandonment. Usually, rafts moved only during daylight hours. By traveling sixty miles a day, not unusual in spring freshet, a raft and crew from Port Jervis could reach Philadelphia in a little over two days; Easton would be an overnight trip. These crews would frequently make another trip or two, or more, before the spring flood subsided. The earliest timber sailors walked home from Philadelphia, stopping at taverns along the way for rest and sustenance. Later crews took a stagecoach or train upriver. Some men served as deckhands aboard ships going from Philadelphia to New York. They would take Hudson River transportation up to Newburg or Kingston, then walk fifty or sixty miles west to their homes in the Delaware Valley.

One maverick rafter liked to travel by moonlight. Elias "Deacon" Mitchell of Callicoon often made the trip from his hometown to Easton without stopping, traveling during periods of full moon. On one occasion, on a bet, he got to Easton from Callicoon in less than a day.

Though high water enabled the rafts to get through the many rapids in the river, the strong current made accidents and loss of life commonplace. Many riverbank dwellers made a good living salvaging and selling derelict rafts and their pieces.

Foul Rift, called the Doomsday Rapids by the initiated, was the most feared stretch of the river. One captain, P. P. Miller, told of his craft taking on a plunging, bucking motion "like a stung horse" when it entered these rapids. A crew member was flung off the bow, and the entire 150-foot raft passed over him. The next thing the captain knew, the lost crew member was clinging to Miller's stern oar, bellowing to be pulled aboard. The man survived, but many were not so fortunate.

Virgil Francisco of Cooks Falls, New York, was on a raft just entering Foul Rift when he observed another craft ahead being driven onto a ledge rock and torn to pieces. "As we passed the accident we could see men struggling in the boiling water—it was a terrifying experience—but we were powerless to stop." He learned later that two of the men drowned.

The section of river at Narrowsburg, New York, proved another challenge. The restricted gap in the mountains here created an extremely swift current; rafts racing forward would often smash into other rafts in the calmer water ahead. Whirlpools were also a problem. A pilot, if not alert, could get trapped in a pool and spend the day literally going around in circles. Worst of all, ice frequently plugged up the narrow gap in early spring, as at least two timber sailors discovered. H. G. Knight collided with an "iceberg" at Narrowsburg during a spring trip, and Frank Walker entered the gap at full speed and was confronted with an ice jam across the entire river. "We staved in the raft and lost it all and climbed a thirty-foot ice bank to get out," he later remembered.

A few miles south at Lackawaxen, Pennsylvania, boats traveling the Delaware and Hudson Canal crossed the river hauling anthracite from the Pennsylvania coal fields. At first, there was no viaduct to carry the canal boats over the river; the vessels simply floated leisurely across to the New York shore, behind a dam built to ensure a pool of water for them. Timber sailors hated the very sight of these intruders and their dam, and if they came upon a boat they never missed an opportunity for a game of tag. Canallers heaved a collective sigh of relief when the company hired John A. Roebling to build an aqueduct over the river in 1848.

In April 1861 Bill Parks, apparently a relative of Skinner's mate, captained a timber leviathan 60 wide and 190 feet long that contained more than 120,000 board feet of lumber. He stopped at Walpack Bend in Sussex County, New Jersey, and put aboard an additional cargo of three thousand five hundred railroad ties of unfloatable green oak. This monster raft, which required a thirteen-man crew, was not unusual on the river at this time. Frequently, large pieces of slate or flagstone from upriver quarries in the Narrowsburg area would be loaded atop the timber and taken to Philadelphia to be used for sidewalks.

With hundreds, even thousands, of the rafts moving on the water at high speeds, conflicts were bound to occur. In 1857 the *Easton Argus* reported a typical incident in which the crews of two rafts opened fire on each other. Five men were shot, and the victors confiscated the tools, weapons, and raft of the losers.

Bridges and other structures posed additional hazards for the timber sailors. Bridges between Phillipsburg and Easton made the river there a real obstacle course. The ironman first had to avoid the piers of the covered Palmer Bridge, whose dangerous lack of headroom at high water caused crew members to duck low or suffer the consequences. This danger passed, the raft would then be buffeted by the powerful current from the Lehigh River, entering from the right. Finally, while he struggled to regain steerage and the raft raced at top speed with the Lehigh's added push, the ironman encountered first one railroad bridge and then another, their piers staggered across the river. The leading edges of these piers were pointed to deflect the force of the water and to break up large pieces of ice that traveled during the spring freshet. These edges could also cut neatly into a fast-moving raft and cause major damage.

Just downstream from the second bridge was a wooden dam built to create a backwater for canal boats to cross the river to the Morris

*The covered Palmer Bridge between Easton and Phillipsburg, view toward Phillipsburg.
This posed a tight squeeze for timber rafts at high water. The bridge was replaced in
1895 by a steel cantilever structure. (Courtesy of Pennsylvania Canal Society Collection,
Hugh Moore Historical Park and Museums, Inc., Easton, Pennsylvania)*

Canal at Phillipsburg. The slow-moving canal boats, laden with Lehigh Valley coal, and the dam over which the rafts catapulted were the final obstacles in this deadly course. Warren Lee, in his book *Down along the Old Bel-Del,* says that in the week of April 18, 1870, twelve rafts were destroyed here. River-watching became a favorite pastime for the good citizens of Phillipsburg and Easton; to be on one of the bridges watching dozens of huge rafts attempt—and sometimes fail—to negotiate this passage was exciting indeed. When sawmills were built in the area, as well as at Belvidere and Portland upstream, many rafts ended their trips before reaching the bridges, much to the relief of captain and crew.

Ferries crossing the river at right angles to raft traffic were always in danger; the rafts had no brakes, and at high water a two-hundred-foot pile of timbers was difficult to steer. The Pike Street Ferry

Artist's depiction of the obstacle course at Phillipsburg and Easton: Palmer Bridge at far right, then the Lehigh River, then the railroad bridge piers. Many rafts were wrecked on this stretch of the river. (Photo courtesy of Ron Wynkoop Sr.)

between Matamoras and Port Jervis was particularly vulnerable and was often near missed and, on occasion, hit. The *Port Jervis Evening Gazette* reported one collision on April 9, 1870, involving a ferry-load of eggs on their way to market; all were lost. Such accidents were common, especially after a severe flood in which bridges washed away and the old ferries were put back into temporary service, often with inexperienced crews.

In April 1869 timberman Frank Walker of Walton, New York, was involved in one of the more humorous incidents on the river. Van Amburg's Circus was traveling by land from Port Jervis to Milford for a performance, but authorities feared that the old covered bridge over the river wouldn't hold the weight of the elephants. The elephants would have to ford the river, it was decided. Walker's raft, when it came upon the wading pachyderms, couldn't avoid them and smashed into one, badly cutting its ear. The wounded elephant, Tippoo Sahib, was a ferocious animal that had recently killed its trainer. Enraged, Tippoo Sahib attempted to climb onto the raft while at the same time blowing water over the crew. The animal's weight totally submerged the stern end of the craft, but a timely jab or two with an oar discouraged the elephant from proceeding further. The traumatized crew escaped unscathed but not unshaken.

At night rafts were anchored in convenient eddies, usually in groups, and sometimes the tethered craft stretched almost across the river. Dingmans Eddy, Upper Black Eddy, and Sandts Eddy were frequently used, as were anchorages at the villages of Milford, Portland, Easton, and New Hope in Pennsylvania; and Delaware Station, Frenchtown, Stockton, and Lambertville in New Jersey. Taverns and hotels opened to accommodate these rough-and-ready timber sailors. Dimmicks Hotel in Milford, Colligan's Stockton Inn, and the Frenchtown Inn catered to these rivermen more than a hundred years ago and are still serving the public today. In her 1873 history of Lambertville, Sarah Gallagher mentioned Stone Tavern as a place where "the watermen are wont to pause to refresh after the perils of the Rocks. . . . The tavern was a great place for card playing, drinking, and fisticuff fighting." An area in South Easton called Snufftown catered to the carnal desires of the sailors; other cities along the way offered similar enticements.

Many raftsmen preferred the less exciting accommodations offered in private homes. Christine Smith, a widow whose Mount Bethel, Pennsylvania, farmhouse bordered the river, welcomed the more sedate sailors who wanted only a good dinner and a spot on her living room floor to bed down. Many farm families living along the river supplemented their incomes this way, and if the meals they offered were good and big enough, they did repeat business.

By 1875 as many as three thousand rafts traveled the river yearly, and in 1880 the *Port Jervis Daily Union* reported that 902 rafts passed through Lackawaxen between January 1 and April 11. Large fleets

Timber raft on the Delaware near Hancock, New York, late nineteenth century. Many of the people are passengers on board for a brief trip. (Courtesy of Pennsylvania Canal Society Collection, Hugh Moore Historical Park and Museums, Inc., Easton, Pennsylvania)

would collect below the Trenton Falls, waiting to be towed by tugs for the final lap to the City of Brotherly Love or even farther downriver to Wilmington, Delaware. But many rafts now completed their journey before even getting to Trenton. Brokers negotiated for timber in Easton and Portland, and, as the growing population along the river needed houses, lumberyards and sawmills sprang up all along the Delaware to meet the demand for lumber. Hagerty's Sawmill in Phillipsburg and Zearfoss-Hilliard Lumber Company at the outlet of Bushkill Creek in Easton were favored by raftsmen because of the excellent docking area for rafts. S. W. Gardner and Company in Belvidere became well known for its pine and hemlock. Lambertville and New Hope became major trading centers, and several sawmills operated in the two towns. John Lequear, writing in the *Hunterdon Democrat* in 1870, noted, "All of the pine lumber that was used in this part of the state was rafted down the Delaware. Hundreds of thousands of feet of lumber were cut here at our mills [in Lambertville] and brought from this place to Plainfield and Somerville. There are hundreds of houses standing there today, the lumber of which was hauled by wagon from Lambertville."

But by the end of the century, commercial timber rafting was on the decline along the Delaware River. The railroads were taking some of this trade (their bridges were also becoming major hazards to the rafts), but more importantly the valley was running out of timber. The diameter of the logs in the rafts became smaller and smaller; all the full-grown trees were gone.

By 1905 timber rafts were a rarity on the river, although newspaper accounts of the great Pumpkin Freshet of 1903 tell of errant rafts destroying bridges along the river (a kind of poetic justice). In 1917, during World War I, a single raft appeared on the river, traveling to Bordentown with logs to be used for pilings. The Delaware Valley and its foothills had become as barren as those English hillsides of the mid-eighteenth century. As Sarah Gallagher wrote of her beloved river valley:

> The hillsides are shorn of their forests,
> Handsome dwellings adorn the plateau.
> What'er was romantic or rustic,
> There is naught of it left, that I know.

4

MR. DURHAM'S
BOAT

n the old days on the Delaware, spring was the time when the upper river came out of hibernation. Ore from the mines, produce from the farms, and fur and timber from the forests had been accumulated during the winter in anticipation of the spring flood. When seasonal rainfall and snowmelt added enough water to the river, timber rafts and other craft started downstream to that eastern metropolis, Philadelphia, where Quaker merchants eagerly bought their goods. Before roads and canals were built, this turbulent waterway offered the only route to the city for upcountry products; river traffic ceased only during the yellow fever epidemic of 1793, when most of Philadelphia's work force died or fled. The early history of the Delaware Valley is primarily a story of river transportation, and the story would be incomplete without mention of that workhorse of the river, the Durham boat.

Robert Durham, an engineer at the Durham Iron Works at Riegelsville, Pennsylvania, designed this boat that conquered the river. He built his prototype in 1757 on the shores of the Delaware near the Durham foundry. This craft carried fifteen tons of pig iron through the rapids of the river to Philadelphia in just two days. The return trip, against the current, took five days. The boat soon became the standard freight hauler of the river, and shipyards such as Thomas Bishop and Son of Easton specialized in its construction. Eventually, the largest fleet of Durhams operated out of Easton, and warehouses lined the city's waterfront on both the Delaware and the Lehigh rivers.

Durham boats were large for Delaware River vessels; the largest measured sixty-five feet long and eight feet in the beam. Pointed at both ends, canoe-like, and without a keel, the craft were propelled with four oars and directed by a long steering oar or "sweep." The boats were open to the sky except for small covered areas in the bow and the stern. Here, some of the crew of four to six men could sleep on straw, protected from the elements. Here, too, were kept the charcoal stove for cooking and warmth, as well as a gallon or two of whiskey or applejack for medical emergencies. The hull, usually painted black, bore the captain's name.

Durham boats could carry up to twenty tons of iron or 150 barrels of flour. When fully loaded the Durhams drew a meager twenty-eight inches of water, and when partially loaded for the return trip they could draw as little as three inches. (This shallow draft was the key to their successful performance through the rapids of the river.) In calm waters, the captain would let the current carry his ship along, guided by only his sweep. Often the craft had a thirty-foot mast and a triangular sail, and a fleet of the boats thus rigged, moving silently and gracefully downstream, offered a beautiful sight and inspiration to many a rustic poet.

Getting these large craft upriver again proved more difficult. They had to be poled against the current, which was especially strong at high water. Two to four men, operating from boards fastened to the inside of each gunwale, pushed with iron-tipped poles against the river bottom or bank. Sometimes the men pulled their boat along by grasping overhead branches, a method called *pulling brush*.

Matthias Cummins, an upcountry man who worked the river, recalled, "We tried to sell the boats at Philadelphia at the end of the

Durham boat. (Photo by Diana Dale)

trip but if we couldn't, we poled them back, getting through Foul Rift with the help of iron rings set in the rocks. We only returned upriver with light loads, mainly sugar and molasses." Those iron rings, driven into the ledges on the Pennsylvania side, were installed in 1791 as part of the project directed by Major Robert Hoops to open Foul Rift to boat traffic (see chapter 3). A crew member would walk along the bank and insert a rope through the nearest ring, then bring the end of the rope back to the boat. The crew would pull the craft upriver through the rapids, then repeat the process with the next ring.

It took a special breed to operate the Durhams up and down the river during spring freshet. The captain was generally a stern task-master, feared and respected by river sailors and landlubbers alike. Many a valley lad dreamed of someday becoming a Durham boat captain, who as a role model was akin to a steamboat captain or loco-motive engineer.

Crew members were less idealized. They were young, often teen-agers, but strong and agile. They worked long, hard days but always had time for a laugh or a practical joke. Timber sailors also were on the river during freshet, and the towns catering to them were lively places, indeed.

Durham boats were so successful that they soon could be found along the entire length of the river, from Hancock to Philadelphia. We know, for example, that by the early 1800s Ebenezer Taylor received goods from Philadelphia, via Durham boat, for his store at Cochecton, New York, a good thirty miles upriver from Port Jervis. Soon, the Durhams spread to other rivers. They carried anthracite coal out of Wilkes-Barre on the Susquehanna, and coal and general produce on the Lehigh. They were even used extensively on the Mohawk River in New York State. For many years the Delaware boats carried iron as their principal product (Pennsylvania ranked as the major iron producing colony and state), but they also carried grain, whiskey, applejack, livestock—virtually anything that needed moving on the river. Van Campen's Mill at Shawnee and Hoops's Mill on the Pequest at Belvidere shipped flour regularly to Philadelphia. The boats even carried river cobbles for paving streets in the growing cities of Philadelphia and Wilmington.

But their most famous exploit was a military one; their most valued cargo, human. George Washington knew about Durham boats. He had seen the huge vessels at the Philadelphia docks when he passed through the city in the summer of 1775, while traveling north to take command of the Continental army surrounding Boston.

By the end of 1776 Washington had returned to the Delaware with his army, now in desperate retreat. He had been outflanked and outfought through New York and across New Jersey, though he always managed to slip away. His army, a few months earlier numbering over twenty thousand men, had dwindled to a sickly and discouraged three thousand. British general Charles Cornwallis had vowed to capture Washington and his army the way "a hunter bags a fox," but he couldn't quite pull it off.

With his back to the river and Cornwallis a mere ten miles away, Washington collected all the Durham boats and other craft for seventy miles and crossed into Pennsylvania at McKonkey's Ferry, upriver from Trenton. Men on the last boat to leave swore they could

Full-size Durham boat replicas in the Delaware at Washington Crossing State Park.
(Photo by Diana Dale)

hear the music of British fifes and drums. A rebel rear guard fired a few rounds of cannon shot back across the river, causing thirteen British casualties. Washington had made it, just barely, with troops, artillery, horses, and ammunition, all packed like cod in the commodius Durhams. He then ordered all the boats hidden or destroyed so the British couldn't follow. Most of the Durhams were secreted behind Malta Island, later called Smith Island, near Lambertville. The British, unable to cross the river, went into various winter encampments in New Jersey, and a large force of Hessian mercenaries settled in at the comfortable village of Trenton. "Civilized" armies, after all, didn't fight in the winter.

But Washington feared that when the river froze solid, the British would cross on the ice and attempt to take Philadelphia. To make matters worse, in just three weeks his troops' enlistments would expire. Because of the privations and hardships his men had suffered, Washington knew few would reenlist. That great propagandist of the

Revolution, Thomas Paine, was there and it was about this situation that he wrote "These are the times that try men's souls." Washington knew he had to act at once. He decided on a Christmas night counterstroke against the Hessians at Trenton.

He planned a pincer movement; General John Cadwalader and General Israel Putnam of Bunker Hill fame would take six hundred soldiers and cross south of Trenton at Bristol and march north. Washington and the remaining two thousand four hundred troops would cross nine miles north of Trenton, at McKonkey's Ferry, and march south. The attack would be made in the dark of night, when the celebrating Hessians should be asleep.

In a raging snow storm, Washington's troops at McKonkey's were carried in Durhams guided by men of the fourteenth Continental Amphibious Regiment (many of whom were black) under the command of Colonel John Glover. Just one of these boats could carry what passed for a complete regiment in the depleted army. As the heavily laden craft, many carrying artillery or horses, went across the river, huge slabs of floating ice threatened to capsize them.

They were no sooner underway than Washington was informed that neither Cadwalader nor Putnam could get across. The ice-filled river at Bristol was much wider than at McKonkey's, and the southern wing, lacking soldiers skilled in boating, couldn't make a landing on the Jersey side. Washington and his little force went on alone.

They got to Trenton on the morning of December 26. The Hessians had already formed for reveille and then gone back to bed, so exhausted were they from the holiday festivities. Washington attacked fiercely with his artillery, his rifles not dependable in the wet snow. (One of the most effective artillery batteries was that of young Captain Alexander Hamilton of New York.) The Hessians fought bravely but were never able to recover from the initial surprise. Of the enemy force of one thousand four hundred troops, four hundred escaped to the south of the city, and the rest were either captured or killed. Washington's casualties consisted of two men wounded and two frozen to death on the march. One of the wounded was a young officer, James Monroe, who would become the fifth president of the

Forty-foot replica of a Durham boat at reenactment of Washington crossing the Delaware. Boat is full size. (Photo courtesy of Washington Crossing Historical Park, Pennsylvania Historical and Museum Commission)

new nation. The victory reversed what, until then, had been a dismal display of retreat and defeat. Flushed with their success, Continental troops readily reenlisted.

In a few days Washington attacked again, this time at Princeton, and here, too, he outmaneuvered the British and won a resounding victory. The British and their Hessian allies retreated to Amboy; Washington's army went into winter quarters at Morristown. Winston Churchill, pretty good at coming from behind himself, described the significance of the victory at Trenton: "The effect of the stroke was out of all proportion to its military importance. It was the most critical moment of the war."

The successes at Trenton and Princeton would have been impossible without the Durham boats. As one crew member put it, albeit with a bit of exaggeration, "The battle was won by Glover and Durham."

Durham boats dominated river transportation well into the nineteenth century. They were the workhorses of the river until they were replaced by canal boats and, later, railroads.

The first canals were built along the river in the 1830s, and the canal boats had an advantage in that they could operate without depending on high water. Also, canals were free of the troublesome obstructions that plagued river traffic. Railroads, of course, contributed to the decline of both Durham boats and canals, giving faster and better service. To the hustling eastern businessman, time was money.

By 1840 Durham boats were disappearing from the river. Many were destroyed during a major flood in January 1841 in which huge chunks of ice smashed everything in their path—including Durham boats moored in eddies and basins. Most of this fleet of river-freight haulers wasn't rebuilt. In an attempt to resurrect declining Durham boat fortunes, Belvidere entrepreneurs in 1844 dug a channel on the Jersey bank, bypassing Foul Rift. They hoped to improve travel time for the boats and, incidentally, to guarantee a constant flow of water to a mill built at the rift. Unfortunately, the channel was not wide enough to accommodate timber rafts. The usefulness of the project was shortlived; the railroads' takeover of commerce along the river could not be deterred. Shortly after the channel opened, the mill was destroyed by fire and not rebuilt.

Later, a Durham captain named Lugar took a load of ships' keels from Portland, Pennsylvania, downriver to the Delaware and Raritan Canal, thence on the canal to New Brunswick, New Jersey, where the boat was towed to the Brooklyn Navy Yard. The boat and its exploits attracted a lot of attention in the New York press, but this was almost the last hurrah for the Durhams. A final trip on the Delaware by a Durham boat was made in March 1860, with Isaac VanNorman commanding.

The Durham's days of glory were over, but this sturdy river craft—designed by an iron monger for use on the most improbable of rivers—made an inestimable contribution to the growth and prosperity of the United States. Philadelphia, the nation's first major city, owed its early survival to the goods brought to it in the hulls of Durham boats. Cities such as Easton, Lambertville, New Hope, and Portland prospered on Durham freight.

Finally, one can't forget the Durhams' essential aid in the victory over the British and Hessians at Trenton. Without Robert Durham's gift on that bitter Christmas season of 1776, the American dream of independence would have died on the frozen banks of the Delaware River.

5

THE RIVER
IN WAR

t be the sole purpose of the army from Canada to effect a junction with General Howe." Such were the instructions that the British colonial secretary, Lord Germain, gave to his commander in Canada. Unfortunately, he didn't have a talk with General Howe.

Specifically, Lord Germain's strategy for the year 1777 was supposed to end the war with the colonies quickly and decisively. British general John "Gentleman Johnny" Burgoyne would lead an army of some eight thousand troops south from Canada along an old American Indian trail, via Lake Champlain and the Hudson River, and meet General "Billy" Howe coming up the Hudson with another army. They would join forces at Albany, defeating any opposition along the way and splitting the colonies in two. This would effectively cut off and isolate that hotbed of the revolution, New England. By the end of the year the war would be over and the American colonies back in the fold. But Howe went to the wrong river.

Howe was obsessed with Philadelphia. He could have gotten there the year before, but Washington and his little army had slammed the door on his fingers at Trenton—some Christmas that

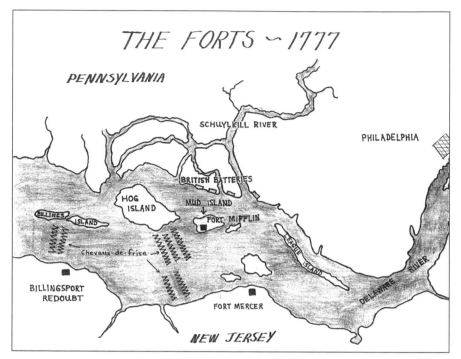

The forts, 1777. (Map courtesy of Diana Dale)

was—and a few days later did it again at Princeton. In June Howe decided he would first attempt to occupy Philadelphia with his army, then send a force to Albany to help Burgoyne. He'd nicely out-flank Washington's army in New Jersey by taking the water route to Philadelphia.

When Howe's transports reached Delaware Bay, however, he was informed that a series of underwater obstructions put in place by the rebels had completely blocked the river. He reversed course, sailed south into Chesapeake Bay, thence north to the head of the Elk River, where he landed his troops. This sorry bunch had been aboard ship for more than a month, crammed below decks in the summer heat. They were happy to get on land again and didn't even mind the sixty-mile march to Philadelphia. Howe had to contend with Washington along the way, at both Brandywine and Germantown, but by the end of September he had arrived in Philadelphia. To get supply ships to his forces in the city, however, Howe would have to clear the river of the obstructions and capture the rebel forts that protected them. In the meantime, Burgoyne had reached the Hudson and was looking for help from downriver.

The underwater obstructions that Howe had to deal with were heavy timbers pointed at one end with iron tips. Rows of these huge spikes were placed in the main channel of the river, each one secured by a rock-filled crib of stones. The points faced downriver and were about four feet underwater, ready to tear open the underside of any war or cargo ship that attempted to pass. Army engineers who were experts in such things called them *chevaux de frise,* since they had been created by the French.

Fourteen miles downriver from the city lay the first set of chevaux de frise. Here, at the settlement of Billingsport, a double row of the pilings spanned the ship's channel, stretching out toward an island called Billings Island. On the Jersey bank stood a small fort, or redoubt, armed with cannon to discourage any tampering. Unfortunately, the fort had never been completed and was lightly held. On October 2, a force of British troops landed downriver from the redoubt and attacked it from the rear. The garrison retreated after spiking the guns. The pilings were cut, and British ships moved on to the next set of chevaux de frise.

Fort Mercer was a mile or two upriver from Billingsport, at a place called Red Bank in New Jersey. Another pick-and-shovel fieldwork, it consisted of trenches and a palisade, and mounted fourteen guns. Between this fort and Fort Mifflin, which stood across the river on Mud Island, stretched two sets of chevaux de frise. Just upriver from these defenses lay a makeshift squadron of naval vessels, including several fire boats and two floating batteries of ten and nine eighteen-pounders respectively, all under the command of a rebel officer, John Hazelwood. The six hundred colonial troops at Fort Mercer were commanded by Colonel Christopher Greene of Rhode Island. Greene, a veteran of Bunker Hill and the terrible march to Quebec with Arnold, was a fighter.

Even though construction of Fort Mercer was incomplete, six hundred men still weren't enough to defend the entire structure. Greene had his men construct a second palisade through the middle of the fort, then moved all of his troops into the southern half.

General Howe elected to have his Hessian troops assault the fort. Colonel Carl von Donop, their commander, had barely escaped capture at the Trenton surprise the previous winter, when he had been forced to abandon all his supplies as well as his sick and wounded. He felt a need to recoup his reputation and that of his Hessian mercenaries. These German hirelings had come to the war with a reputation of Germanic invincibility but their ignominious defeat at Trenton had made them something of a laughingstock. Now von Donop's forces outnumbered the Americans two-to-one.

On October 23 the Hessians crossed the Delaware upriver from the fort and approached it from the northeast. The land around the palisades had been cleared, so the colonial troops could observe the approach and prepare for the attack. Von Donop sent an officer under a flag of truce to offer Greene an opportunity to surrender. Greene refused. The attack was begun about four in the afternoon, which in October left little daylight. The Hessians advanced in their usual aligned manner and, with the help of ladders they carried with them, crossed the trenches and scaled the first palisade. The attackers had entered the part of the fort abandoned by Greene's men; believing victory was theirs, they cheered and threw their hats in the air. Their joy was short-lived. The defenders rose up from the second palisade and began firing. The slaughter was prodigious.

The British made another attempt from the south side of the fort. This force, observing the retreat of the first group, lost heart and didn't persevere. A third attack was mounted; this assault came under the fire of the two floating batteries in the river, and was repulsed. British warships attempted to close in and intervene. Two ran aground after dark attempting to avoid the chevaux de frise and weren't discovered until the next morning. The *Augusta* caught fire as a result of the American bombardment and blew up; the *Merlin* was destroyed by its own crew. The *Augusta,* mounting sixty-four guns, was the

Trenches at Fort Mercer. (Photo by Diana Dale)

pride of the British Delaware fleet and its loss was especially humili-
ating. It was the largest British warship to be destroyed by the Americans in the entire war.

As darkness fell, the cries, in German, of the wounded and dying
chilled the air. Fatally wounded, von Donop would die within days
and be buried in an unmarked grave near the fort. Twenty-two of his
officers, including all of his battalion commanders, were casualties.
Five hundred of his men were killed, wounded, or captured. Among
the Americans, fourteen were killed and twenty-three wounded. Fort
Mercer remained in American hands. At about this time news from
Saratoga arrived; Burgoyne could no longer await assistance and had
surrendered his entire army.

Fort Mifflin stood across from Fort Mercer on Mud Island, separated from the Pennsylvania shore by only a narrow channel. Mud Island was well named, since it was simply a mud flat that would have
been underwater at high tide had it not been for the dike surrounding it. Most of the earthworks and buildings of the fort had been

The explosion of the British sixty-four-gun frigate Augusta *and the burning of the eighteen-gun* Merlin *during the bombardment of Fort Mercer on October 23, 1777. (Courtesy of Independence Seaport Museum, Philadelphia)*

built by the Americans under the guidance of a young French engineer named Louis Fleury. The fortifications were occupied by about five hundred men, some of them veterans of the Saratoga fighting. On November 10, Howe began a bombardment of the island from the Pennsylvania shore, as well as from nearby islands at the mouth of the Schuylkill River and from British ships on the Delaware. The shelling continued for a full week, day and night. The defenders got no sleep and almost no food, and worked desperately during lulls in the fighting to repair the damage. Among their defenses the Americans had a thirty-two-pound cannon that had fired off all its shot. The British had a cannon of similar caliber firing at the fort. The American commander offered a gill of rum to any soldier who could recover a cannonball and bring it to the American weapon. Private

Monument commemorating the successful defense of Fort Mercer against the Hessian attackers. (Photo by Diana Dale)

Joseph Martin was there and wrote in his diary: "I saw from twenty to fifty men standing on the parade ground waiting with impatience the coming of the shot which would often be seized before its motion had fully ceased. When the lucky fellow who had caught it had swallowed his rum, he would return to wait for another."

On November 15 British warships entered the narrow channel behind the island; the chevaux de frise had been washed away by an unusually strong current. Private Martin counted six ships with more than one hundred guns firing at close quarters, in addition to the guns on shore. The barrage pulverized the island fortress. That night the Americans abandoned Fort Mifflin. Martin, one of the last to leave, noted the destruction seen by the light of burning buildings: "The whole area of the fort was completely ploughed as a field. The buildings of every kind were hanging in broken fragments, and the guns all dismounted, and how many of the garrison sent to the world of the spirits, I know not. If ever destruction was complete, it was here." The survivors left in boats, still under fire, and escaped to Fort Mercer.

With Fort Mifflin in British hands, the British ships had free use of the Delaware and could supply Howe's army in Philadelphia. There was no point now in the Americans keeping Fort Mercer, and they abandoned it on the night of November 20. To capture these forts, the British had paid a high price. Howe, because he had remained for so long on this river attempting to conquer the stubborn rebels, had let Burgoyne's army be destroyed on the banks of the Hudson. Success at Saratoga would have been much more important to Britain's cause than the conquest of three earthworks on the Delaware River. The rebels' victory at Saratoga and their dogged defense of the Delaware forts convinced the French government that the American army, with a little help, had both the will and the skill to win the war. The French also became convinced that the Revolution was no mere regional uprising of New England malcontents; at Red Bank, Rhode Island troops fought on Jersey soil under a Virginian commander to defend a Pennsylvania city. The ensuing

French alliance with the colonies led ultimately to the final victory at Yorktown.

After the fighting at the forts, Washington's army went into winter quarters at Valley Forge. On his arrival there, Private Martin wrote: "I had nothing to do but make out my supper as usual, upon a leg-of-nothing and no turnips."

It would be a long war.

6

MASSACRE AT MINISINK

errorism is nothing new. In the American Revolution, as British military fortunes declined, the British war ministry began to heed the advice of the governor of New York, Lord Tryon, to "loose the savages against the miserable Rebels in order to impose a reign of terror on the frontiers." Irregular units composed of the fierce Iroquois (and often a few Loyalists disguised as Iroquois) began attacking frontier settlements and individual farms in New York and Pennsylvania. The British offered eight dollars for a scalp and were not particular whether it came from a man, a woman, or a child.

Joseph Brant was the feared and capable leader of these units. He has been characterized in the pages of history as a blood-thirsty monster. Vernon Leslie, Minisink historian, was probably closer to the truth when he wrote: "Brant was a comparatively humane Indian leader within the framework of the period in which he lived."

A Mohawk of the Iroquois family, Brant early in life came under British influence. He was a protégé of Sir William Johnson, superintendent of Indian affairs in British North America (some believe Brant was Johnson's illegitimate son) and fought under Johnson as a thirteen-year-old in the French and Indian War, at which time he took his first scalp. As a youth he joined the Church of England and received his education, including a proficiency in Latin and Greek, at the Moor Charity School, later known as Dartmouth College. In 1775 he visited England and, with his flawless English and handsome mien, was treated with cordiality and respect, had his portrait painted by George Romney, and was presented at Court. In early 1776 he returned to an America in revolt. Now holding a royal commission as colonel in the British Army, he was appointed leader of the Iroquois forces arrayed against American revolutionists on the frontier.

As Brant's forces went into action, rumors of atrocities spread, and whether true or not they struck fear into the hearts of frontier families. Farmers went to their fields in armed groups and kept their cattle under guard. Certain homes in the communities were fortified with palisades and stocked with food to serve as forts in the event of attack. One of the most devastating raids took place in the Wyoming Valley of the Susquehanna River near Wilkes-Barre, Pennsylvania. Here, civilians and militia were massacred with only slight losses among the attackers. Tales of scalping and of civilians being burned alive made this raid a byword for Iroquois brutality. Brant led an attack a month later on a place called Cherry Valley, twenty-five miles west of Albany. Here, too, a small militia force proved ineffectual against the eight hundred attackers. The entire settlement was burned and about forty civilians were killed, with another seventy-one taken captive. A Boston newspaper reported a survivor's account: "Robert Henderson's head was cut off, his skull bone cut out with his scalp—Mr. Willis's sister was rip't up, a child of Mr. Willis's, two months old, scalp't and arm cut off, the clergyman's wife's leg and arm cut off." Six months later Brant and his force arrived on the banks of the Delaware at a place called Minisink.

The name Minisink referred to an area around the confluence of the Neversink and Delaware Rivers—modern Port Jervis—and buildings here have been identified as targets of the attack. Continental troops under General Pulaski had been stationed here through the winter but had been withdrawn to escort to Easton British captured at the Battle of Stony Point. Brant struck on July 20, 1779. Reporting later on the raid, he described his dissatisfaction. He arrived at noon rather than in the early morning, and the cattle were already in the woods and difficult to find. He complained that he did not get more scalps, that the settlers quickly ran to a fortified house "like ground-hogs." He then added: "We have burnt all the settlement except one fort [fortified house] which we lay before an hour. We destroyed several stockades and forts, took four scalps and three prisoners." Brant and his force started upriver the next morning along a trail on the east bank of the Delaware (the approximate location of modern Route 97). Encumbered with booty, stolen cattle, and prisoners, they moved slowly.

That evening, fugitives from Brant's attack reached the village of Goshen, home base for the Third Regiment of Orange County Militia. The regular commander of the regiment had been captured by the British; his adjutant, Lieutenant Colonel Benjamin Tusten, was in command. Tusten acted quickly. He sent word of the attack to militia groups in Warwick and in Sussex County, New Jersey. The groups were to meet the following morning at Minisink. The next day, at midmorning, a force of about eighty militia met. In addition to Tusten's group, there were members of the Second Regiment of Sussex County under Major Samuel Meeker, and members of an Ulster county militia regiment. This quasi-military force was armed but had little ammunition or food. On learning that Brant's force had departed only that morning, most of the men were anxious to follow.

Tusten, the ranking officer, urged caution. As Goshen's leading physician, Tusten was admired and respected in the area, and undoubtedly his rank reflected this respect rather than his military skills. Yet considering the imagined superiority in numbers of Brant's force and the limited ammunition of the militia, his caution was warranted. Meeker, however, insisted on immediate pursuit. His admonition, "Let the brave men follow me; the cowards may stay behind," could not be denied. As they were about to leave, members of the fourth regiment of Orange County appeared, under the command of Colonel John Hathorn. This addition of 40 men brought the force to a total of 120.

Hathorn, the highest ranking officer, took charge. The new commander conceded to Meeker's demand for immediate action. He decided to take a parallel trail on the hillside above Brant's forces and, by sheer exertion, get ahead of them. He would then cut down to the river trail and set up an ambush. The militia left in hot pursuit.

That night Brant's troops camped on Halfway Brook, sight of present-day Barryville, about fifteen miles from Minisink. The militia, moving rapidly on the upper trail until midnight, had gone almost as far, to a place called Skinner's Sawmill. Next morning they continued the race.

Brant knew of the upper trail—he had local loyalists in his force—and anticipated a possible attack. He sent two loyalists, one of whom was Mowberry Owens, a rebel deserter, to scout the upper trail. When the two didn't return, Brant assumed they had been killed or captured, thus confirming the presence of militia. Actually, Owens had deserted his Iroquois friends and would later rejoin his Continental regiment. After the war Owens settled in Warwick, his reputation apparently unsullied by the fact that he had changed sides twice during the war.

Brant's force was now nearing the ford in the Delaware at Lackawaxen, where they would cross into Pennsylvania and safety. He pushed the column hard. In the lead were prisoners under guard and captured cattle, and they entered the river cautiously. Brant's warriors, the rear guard, were some four hundred yards behind. But Hathorn's force had reached the high ground overlooking the crossing and opened fire on the men in the river.

Brant, in a report of the battle, describes what happened next: "I immediately marched up a hill in their rear with forty men & came around on their backs. . . . The rebels soon retreated and I pursued them until they stopt upon a Rocky Hill round which we were employed & very busy near four hours." In the dash to the hill many militia members deserted and didn't take part in the fighting. Probably only about 60 of the original 120 remained for the final battle.

Once on the hill, the militia formed into a square. John Knap, a survivor, describes what happened: "All that could be done was to face the enemy all around us . . . flat stones were set up edgewise for our defence. . . . Col. Thurston with us was a surgeon and to him the wounded repaired in the centre." The fighting lasted almost until dusk. As the militia took heavy casualties, ammunition and water were running out. To conserve ammunition, Hathorn ordered his men to fire only when certain of a hit. This lull in the firing encouraged the Iroquois and in the twilight they rushed the square and overwhelmed it. The survivors ran if they could. Knap remembered: "We all fled, the officers called out stand, stand, but none would. I heard the wounded beg of us not to leave them and ere I was out of hearing I heard some begging of the Indians to spare their lives." Knap left two uncles on the hill, both fellow soldiers; they were killed, as was his company commander, Captain John Little. Knap, his brother, and others ran to the river and waded across at the ford. The Iroquois fired at them and Knap's brother was hit, but he continued on. Although most of the survivors escaped by crossing the river and going downstream through the dense woods, a few hid in the woods on the New York side. Some were discovered and killed; others avoided detection in the dark. Major Samuel Meeker and an aide, Captain Joseph Harker of Harker's Hollow, New Jersey, both walking wounded, got back alive. Six of the eleven identifiable members of the Second Sussex County Regiment were killed. Captain John Wood, from one of the Orange County regiments, was wounded and captured, the only prisoner taken. He was released at war's end after four years' captivity in Canada.

Colonel Hathorn suffered three minor wounds and managed to escape. As he left the hill he bade farewell to Tusten, who as a surgeon chose to remain with the wounded. A temporary shelter had been set up under a ledge on the battlefield, and here Tusten stayed with seventeen of the most seriously wounded. Brant's men killed them all and took their scalps.

The total number of militia soldiers killed in the Battle of Minisink exceeded forty, although the exact number will never be known. Brant, in his report of the battle, said, "We have taken forty

The monument at Goshen, New York, commemorating those who died in the Minisink massacre. (Photo by Diana Dale)

odd scalps and one prisoner." His own casualties, he said, were three killed and ten wounded, several of the wounded dying later. Militia survivors insisted that Brant's figures relating to his own casualties were too low.

Two days after the defeat, a force was sent from Goshen to recover the American bodies and the wounded, if any, and to attack the Iroquois. There is some indication that several wives of the missing were in this group. When this force neared the battlefield, a heavy rainstorm struck and made their firearms and powder useless. Defenseless, the group returned to Goshen.

No further attempt was made to return to the site of the massacre for more than forty years, and the bodies remained undisturbed by all but the forest animals. Hathorn, who had been promoted to major general, became a prominent politician after the war, serving in the U.S. House of Representatives. Strangely, he made no attempt, official or unofficial, to reclaim the bodies of his comrades-in-arms.

Finally, in April 1822, after a biography of Colonel Tusten had renewed interest in the affair, a party set out from Goshen to bring the bodies home. They had no trouble locating the battlefield, although it was overgrown. They collected a large wagonload of bones, most on the battlefield but some at a distance. One skeleton was found in a rock crevice, a wounded man who had apparently crawled there and died. On July 22, 1822, the bones were interred under a fine monument in a Goshen cemetery. At the ceremony before a large crowd and a contingent of West Point cadets, Major General Hathorn, the guest of honor, laid the cornerstone.

In 1861 the monument was vandalized and had to be replaced through funds contributed by the public. Today this white marble marker still stands, though two of its four marble eagles (one at each corner of the base) have been stolen. In 1929 a second monument was erected, this one on the battlefield itself. It contained three bronze plaques listing the names of the dead. All of the plaques have been stolen, as have the aluminum signs installed to replace them. *Sic Transit Gloria.*

7

THE FIRST
STEAMBOAT

ccentric? The word was invented for this man. Trenton's John Fitch was alcoholic, bigamous, and suicidal. He thought he was going insane, and he was probably correct. But between drinks and bouts with dementia, he built and operated steamboats on the Delaware River decades before anyone *heard* of Robert Fulton and his *Clermont*.

Born in Connecticut in 1743, Fitch followed a variety of callings as a youth. He mined and sold potash, learned something of the silversmith's art, became an expert on rifles, and picked up the rudiments of surveying. He married and had two children, then decided sexual abstinence was necessary for his mental well-being. Mrs. Fitch apparently disagreed and the marriage deteriorated. The couple separated but never divorced.

Fitch came to Trenton around 1765 and worked in a silversmith's shop. Pieces of his work still exist, and they indicate a fine artisan. Before long he owned the shop, and by the time of the American Revolution he was a wealthy and respected businessman. That prosperity grew when he won a contract to manufacture muskets for the militia. His factory with twenty employees was one of the city's largest. When the British occupied Trenton in December 1776, Fitch escaped across the Delaware to Philadelphia, taking with him a fortune in silver and gold. When the British occupied Philadelphia the following year he fled to Lancaster, Pennsylvania, after burying most of his treasure on a friend's farm for safe-keeping. When Washington went into winter quarters at Valley Forge, Fitch was there— with a Conestoga wagon full of liquor to sell to the troops. Business boomed.

When the British evacuated Philadelphia, Fitch returned to the area to retrieve his treasure, only to find it gone; somebody had discovered his hiding place. For his work producing rifles for the army, Fitch had been paid in Continental paper currency, which became almost worthless after the war. Destitute, Fitch went west to the Ohio River valley in 1780 to search for land on the new frontier. In Kentucky he surveyed several plots of land that appealed to him, then returned to Philadelphia and filed a claim for them with the U.S. Congress. On his way back to Kentucky on an Ohio River flatboat, Fitch and his party were taken captive by hostile Delaware Indians.

While captive, Fitch noticed the efficiency and speed with which several of his captors, paddling in unison, could move a canoe through the water, even against the current. He was aware of the steam engine—Watt's invention was known among educated people throughout the world—and understood its mechanics. At nights, he designed in his mind a steam-powered boat.

Fitch was finally sold by his captors to the British at Detroit. He had been virtually adopted by his captor, Chief Buffalo, and the chief's wife, and Fitch departed from his new family with some reluctance. On his return to the new United States, Fitch designed and built a model steamboat. He presented his idea to members of the Continental Congress in Philadelphia, hoping to secure an exclusive patent, but the members rejected his petition. Furious, he referred to them in his candid autobiography as "a bunch of boys" and stated that he had additional motivation now—"to prove them blockheads." Fitch then took his model to that great scientist/inventor, Benjamin

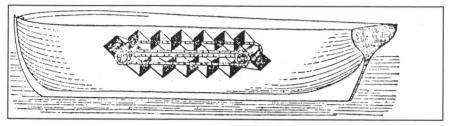

Model of Fitch's steam propulsion device: a series of paddles fastened to an endless chain.
(From Dunbar's A History of Travel in America*)*

Franklin, sure of a sympathetic endorsement. Instead, Franklin rebuffed him with "it will never prove practical." Fitch added another blockhead to his list.

But Fitch persevered. He took on as a partner the hard-drinking but capable Henry Voight, another Philadelphian, and the two of them formed the Steam Boat Company with three hundred dollars in working capital. They produced a prototype that they launched on the Delaware River at Philadelphia in July 1786. The craft measured a mere forty-five feet long and was propelled by a paddle wheel. The engine and firewood took up most of the available space, with hardly enough room left for the proud inventors. The boat roared, smoked, and fizzled, terrifying the crowd of onlookers—but it didn't move. After some fruitless tinkering, the humiliated Fitch took his idea back to the drawing board, but only after an interval in which, as he later wrote, he made himself "pretty free with some West India rum."

Fitch now used a method of propulsion he first noticed while a captive on the Ohio River. He replaced the paddle wheel with two rows of mechanical paddles connected to steam-powered shafts. On August 22, 1787, with many members of the Constitutional Convention present, Fitch launched his second boat at Philadelphia. This craft attained a speed of eight miles per hour and ran successfully up-river to Bordentown, New Jersey, against on outgoing tide. It mattered not that the engine's boiler sprang a leak at the conclusion of the test run; Fitch's steamboat was a success. He began carrying passengers across the river on a regular basis.

Fitch's third model placed three upright paddles in the stern. In the summer of 1789 this steam packetboat began making regular trips between Philadelphia and Trenton. (From Dunbar's A History of Travel in America*)*

With this triumph Fitch was able to gain additional financing. He and Voight designed and built a larger craft, propelled by three paddles in the stern, which they christened the *Experiment*. The craft became a commercial carrier on both the Delaware and the Schuylkill rivers.

But John Fitch's days of glory were brief. In his lifetime, steamboats on the Delaware were never more than a novelty. Every accident or breakdown met with derision. He was looked upon as an eccentric, something his personal life seemed to affirm, and his few backers were considered incompetent businessmen. Money was always in short supply. He tried to convince the federal government to build steamboats for the Ohio and Hudson rivers, but to no avail. At his own expense he built a boat for the Ohio; on its first trip it ran aground in a storm and was wrecked. Fitch lost everything.

He then went to France to seek financial help. While there he became friendly with Aaron Vail, the U.S. consul, and gave Vail drawings and specifications for a proposed craft (some of these specifications were later used by Robert Fulton). France, however, was in the throes of its own revolution, and no government official had time for Fitch. The inventor returned to the United States empty-handed.

Fitch's personal life deteriorated rapidly. He became a derelict, roaming the streets aimlessly. Always a heavy drinker, Fitch and his partner frequented a local tavern and were served by a particularly pretty woman named Mary Krafft. She became pregnant by Voight, who was already married and the father of a large family. According to Fitch, "I said to my male friend, 'I will marry the woman and pledge my word of honor never to bed with her.'" Although he had never divorced his first wife, Fitch married Mary Krafft and the two lived together in rooms above the tavern where she worked.

The arrangement was fraught with turmoil. Fitch and a jealous Voight battled frequently over the woman, although Fitch probably kept his word and abstained from having sex with her, and after several months Krafft ended the marriage and moved away. In 1796, at the age of fifty-three, Fitch drifted to Kentucky, to the area where he had worked years before as a surveyor and where he owned some land. He moved into a tavern in Bardstown, Kentucky, where he signed over land to the tavern keeper and lived out his remaining days. He died on July 2, 1798, from an overdose of whiskey and opium. It would be nine years before Robert Fulton, drawing on Fitch's expertise, would launch the *Clermont* on the Hudson River.

Years later Connecticut, the birth state of John Fitch, placed on the east wall of the state capitol a bronze tablet that read: "John Fitch—first in the world's history to invent and apply steam propulsion of vessels through water." And at Trenton, on the banks of his beloved Delaware, on John Fitch Way, a memorial plaque placed in 1921 honors the man whose crude steamboat was the first one to navigate on this or any other river.

8

STANDOFF AT LACKAWACK

hink of a log raft the size of a football field riding spring floodwaters down the twisting Delaware, with no way to stop—and with little steerage to boot. In the heyday of timber rafting, such rafts crowded the river, one never out of view of others on their way to Philadelphia, Easton, or Lambertville. In a season of only four or five raftworthy freshets, as many as three thousand of the craft made the trip.

There were some especially dangerous areas for rafts on the river. The natural obstructions at Skinners Falls, Foul Rift, and Wells Falls, or the piers at Easton, took all of a steersman's know-how—and a prayer from the rest of the crew—to get past. But none were more dreaded by timber sailors than the obstructions at Lackawaxen, where the Delaware and Hudson Canal crossed the river.

This canal, opened in 1829, was created to carry clean-burning anthracite coal from the mines of northeastern Pennsylvania to the Hudson River at Kingston, thence downriver to New York City. Even before the canal was finished, though, it tormented the timber sailors. Much of the canal ditch was built parallel and close to the Delaware

River, and fun-loving Irish construction crews timed their blasts to shower passing rafts with rocks and dirt. At the Delaware they built a seven-foot-high wooden dam; this dam created a pool that enabled the heavy-laden coal scows to cross the river, even in periods of low water. The mules, which powered the boats on the canal, were ferried over separately. At the pool, a hawser stretched from the Pennsylvania to the New York banks; the canaller simply pulled his craft across to the lock on the other side, then harnessed up his mules again and proceeded on his way. If a canal boat entered the river with sufficient headway, the canaller would often ignore the hawser and free-float to the other side, using his boat's momentum. Either way, the crossing process was a slow one.

Rafters had been using the river to haul timber to the Philadelphia shipyards since Callicoon's Daniel Skinner made the first trip in 1764. An experienced ironman knew, or thought he knew, every rift, eddy, rock, and other obstruction along the way. One can only imagine his consternation when, at race-course speed and with no way to stop, he found in his path a two-inch-thick hawser line, several fully loaded coal boats traveling at a snail's pace, and just beyond that a dam with spring flood waters surging over its top.

Accidents became commonplace. Rafts collided with canal boats, rafts collided with each other trying to avoid canal boats, and many rafts fell apart going over the dam. Leslie Wood, in his classic *Rafting on the Delaware River,* described this last situation:

> The forward end of the raft floated out a few feet in midair and then suddenly plunged down into the water below, the raft bending in the middle from the force of gravity on both ends, and the forward oarsmen, who sometimes stood two feet in water when the raft plunged, were hidden from the sight of those on the rear end. A tremendous pressure was exerted on all parts of the craft when going over the dam, the whole framework creaking and groaning like a huge monster in terrible agony.

If the raft survived the dam, as soon as it reached calm water a crew member would take an axe, plugs, and spikes and go over the raft, making needed repairs.

To the timber sailors this situation was intolerable, and as early as April 1829 the *Easton Argus* reported: "A public meeting was held by those who considered themselves aggrieved, and a representation sent to the managers that if the obstruction was not immediately removed, they would remove it by force. The request was not complied with, and they accordingly proceeded to the dam, blew it up and tore away about eighty feet of it, and succeeded in clearing a passage for their rafts."

Canal crews quickly restored the dam, but they added a chute on the Pennsylvania side intended to make passage by the rafts easier. This gesture by the canal company improved things slightly—if the raft's pilot could locate the chute in the confusion of high water and rambling canal boats—but the raftsmen still looked upon the canallers as trespassers. Individual confrontations between the two occurred daily during the rafting season; violent imprecations-of which the timber sailors were masters—were answered by missles of hard coal. In a test of strength, however, the slow-moving canal boat proved no match for an onrushing log mammoth. In addition to absorbing the costs of damages to its own equipment, the canal company was in constant litigation with timber companies, and it usually lost.

The profitability of the Delaware and Hudson Canal increased every year. In 1839 the canal moved 122,300 tons of coal to Kingston, and in just two years that figure grew to 192,200 tons. In 1842 the sides of the canal were raised so that more heavily laden boats could be used. By 1847 the canal was moving 500,000 tons of coal a year and was fast becoming a financial bonanza to its stockholders. The claims of the timber interests were petty compared to the profits to be made from getting the coal to New York City, and canal management went to great lengths to pacify the timber people. But this increase in business meant more and larger canal boats crossing at Lackawaxen— and more complaints by the timber interests. Some of the Pennsyl-

vania legislators who had granted permission for the dam began to
have second thoughts.

In February 1830 Philip Hone, president of the Delaware and
Hudson Canal Company, met with the timbermen and state legislators and viewed the obstructions at Lackawaxen. Apparently Hone
made some kind of accommodation or promise, for the legislators returned to Harrisburg without recommending any changes. In truth,
canal management had become disenchanted with the Lackawaxen
crossing. In addition to the constant repairs to the dam necessitated
by raft and ice damage, the crossing had become a serious bottleneck.
During the season canal boats almost always backed up in the Pennsylvania locks leading to the Delaware, as well as at the ferry and the
hawser crossings. The company decided that the Lackawaxen crossing would have to be done away with.

In February 1846 management authorized the building of an aqueduct one hundred feet downriver from the dam to carry canal boats
over the Delaware. The contractor, John A. Roebling, finished the
six-hundred-foot suspension bridge in 1848, and it began operation
by the following spring. This aqueduct was one of several Roebling
built to improve the capacity of the canal. Later in life he would use
the experience gained here to build the Brooklyn Bridge.

Although the aqueduct eliminated the bottleneck at the old river
crossing, life did not get easier for the timber sailors. The new structure placed in the river three large masonry and stone piers, each
132 to 142 feet apart. For a pilot, dodging these piers with a two-
hundred-foot raft in high water was almost as bad as dodging the
canal boats. And the hated dam was still in place. To make matters
worse, the canal company decided to raise the dam to sixteen feet,
more than double its original height, and use it to feed the canal in its
run down to Port Jervis.

To compensate for this, the canal company built a chute through
the center of the dam with wings extending upriver several hundred
feet. If the steersman entered the chute properly, and was not turned
by the wind, he would exit the chute aimed directly at the opening
between the two center piers of the aqueduct. A piece of log was

John A. Roebling's aqueduct carried canal boats above the river, keeping them out of the way of timber rafts, but its piers posed new obstacles. (Photo courtesy of the Minisink Valley Historical Society, Port Jervis, New York)

anchored in the river in direct line with the chute, and the timber sailors soon learned to pass over this buoy to be in correct alignment.

At the beginning, the company hired skilled river pilots, at a generous ten dollars a day, to guide the rafts through the chute and under the aqueduct. A pilot would board a raft near the mouth of the Lackawaxen and help steer the raft through the obstacle course. Then he would return upriver in a small boat.

As the timber sailors became more adept at conquering these obstacles, the canal company modified this expensive operation. In *Rafting Story of the Delaware,* Joshua Pine wrote in 1883: "The company built a house on the bank . . . which is occupied by an agent [called a

A raft goes through the chute at Lackawaxen Dam, on the Delaware River. (Photo courtesy of the Minisink Valley Historical Society, Port Jervis, New York)

tallyman] who asks the name of the owner of every craft that passes, the name of the steersman and directs him how, when, and where to pull and how to run. . . . A raft gets stove against the piers occasionally but the company pays all charges."

By this time a telegraph had been installed along the canal, and any accident or loss would be wired back to the home office for quick action on a settlement.

Any raftsman worth his salt had to be adaptable to the vagaries of river operation. Although timber sailors never fully accepted this blockage to their river, they learned to live with it. When a new generation of rafters came along, one that had never known the river without the dam and aqueduct, they accepted these objects as a matter of course. The *Middletown Daily Record* reported that in 1875, 3,140 rafts passed through the dam and under the aqueduct. In 1880 a tallyman at the dam reported that 390 rafts passed over the dam during a single freshet; all escaped damage. Some of these rafts carried, in addition to their usual load, high stacks of flagstone and other products from upriver quarries. In 1870 a timber raft that Charles Curtis remembered in his book, *Rafting on the Delaware,* as "the largest raft ever to float on the river," measured 201 feet by 75 feet. On top of the raft's structural timber were piled several thousand feet of heavy hardwood planks. This monster required eight oarsmen who managed to take it through the dam and under the aqueduct and thence to Philadelphia without incident.

By this time, however, timbermen had to deal with other problems. River hillsides had been stripped bare, and marketable trees were becoming more and more difficult to find within reach of the river. Before long, concerns about obstacles in the river became moot. By the end of the century, the timber was gone—and so was the canal.

9

GETTER'S ISLAND

he island sits in the Delaware opposite the mouth of the Bushkill River at Easton. It's not much more than a teardrop-shaped sand bar, its twisted trees scarred by river ice and festooned with debris from recent freshets. Years ago the place was called Abel Island, some believed in commemoration of that first of all murders. Actually, the place was named for a respected local family who listed the island among its extensive land holdings. The island's association with murder—and its present name—didn't occur until long after that original crime, in 1833.

Young Carl Getter was a recent German immigrant who found employment as an itinerant laborer with farmers in the Easton area. His agricultural skills and rugged physique kept him regularly working. He apparently was regularly active with women as well, especially in the winter when a slow-down in farmwork left extra time for romantic pursuits. On January 19, 1833, Carl was charged by Margaret Lawall with being the father of her unborn child. Whether or not he admitted to fatherhood we don't know, but the Easton magistrate gave him a choice of marriage or prison. He chose the former as the easiest way out of his predicament. It proved to be his undoing.

Although Carl married Margaret, he couldn't abide her and, to quote the sensational press of the day, refused "to set up housekeeping." He continued to savor the joys of single blessedness and soon formed an association with one Molly Hummer. Carl could abide Molly quite well, and he determined to end his brief marriage. On the frozen morning of February 28, the body of Margaret Lawall Getter was found in a limestone quarry about three miles from Easton. The woman, presumably still carrying the unborn child, had been choked to death. Police arrested Getter the same day and put him in the old Easton lockup. He was indicted in the Court of Oyer and Terminar and went on trial in August.

In the long interval between arrest and trial, the local press served up the crime's lurid details and whipped the readership into a frenzy with daily updates. Margaret's murder became the area's most sensational crime. Getter was represented in court by James Porter, a prominent local criminal lawyer, but even Porter could not save the hapless farmhand, already condemned by press and readers alike. Carl Getter was sentenced to be hanged, the date of execution set for October 31.

Because of the intense public interest in the case, the execution took place on Abel's Island. Though the island sits low in the river, both riverbanks opposite the island are high, forming a natural amphitheater ideal for accommodating huge crowds. By October 30, spectators filled every hotel and boardinghouse in Easton. Still, all night and into the next day crowds continued to pour into the city and into Phillipsburg across the river. The perfect weather heightened the festiveness. Hawkers offered for sale pictures of Getter as well as pamphlets containing a full account of the trial in both German and English. The *Easton Sentinel* estimated that an astounding one hundred thousand spectators had arrived to witness the execution. The occasion could be compared only to something the early Romans contrived when feeding Christians to the lions.

Shortly after 1:00 P.M. the doors of the ancient prison opened and the prisoner, dressed in a white suit, appeared. He was accompanied by some friends, the sheriff, and a clergy member, the Reverend Hecht. Those who knew the prisoner before his incarceration were surprised at his appearance. Getter had gained considerable weight while in

The old Easton jail in Easton, Pennsylvania. Here Getter was held until he was hanged.
(Photo courtesy of Ron Wynkoop Sr.)

prison, and he told waiting friends that he had slept well. Now, wearing the white suit, he looked like a prosperous banker; several onlookers mistook him for the sheriff.

Although offered a cart for his last journey, Getter chose to walk to the island. The reporter for the *Sentinel* noted that the prisoner, although manacled, strolled leisurely to his fate. The procession included a carriage with five physicians and a cart carrying the coffin, with a troop of cavalry providing escort through the mob and over a bridge of boats to the gallows. The same reporter noted the prisoner's care to avoid getting his feet wet. The press also made much of the gallows and its design in the latest New York style; instead of dropping through a trap door, the prisoner was yanked upward by heavy weights attached to the other end of the execution rope. After prayers by the Reverend Hecht, Getter bid farewell to friends and acquaintances (including Margaret's brother, with whom he had developed a friendship). After affirming he was ready, he stepped to the gallows, calmly assisted in adjusting a hood and noose over his head, shook hands with the sheriff—and was hanged.

"He had scarcely been raised three feet from the ground," wrote the *Sentinel* reporter, "when the rope snapped off and he fell." (So much for New York design.) Getter lay unconscious briefly but then revived. He looked up at the broken rope and, with a wry smile, remarked, "That was good for nothing." The crowd remained silent at the chilling scene as Getter stood up holding a bruised arm. He leaned against the gallows while the sheriff and deputy decided how to handle this unusual situation. Finally the deputy went off to find a more reliable piece of rope while the prisoner continued his wait. After some time the deputy returned, and Getter watched with interest as the new rope was fastened to the weights and then to his bruised neck. The job done, he stepped to the gallows, shook hands all around, and was hanged again. He lived for eleven minutes suspended in the air, quivering slightly. Then all motion ceased. After thirty minutes he was cut down and placed in the new coffin, which was handed over to relatives.

Thus ended somewhat morosely the life of Carl Getter. Yet he achieved in death not only notoriety for the murder, but also fame for his calmness in the face of his especially trying death. He also gained a form of immortality, as the place of his execution was known from that day on as Getter's Island.

The island would be the site of yet another tragedy thirty years later when the steamboat *Alfred Thomas* exploded on its shore. From this catastrophe—the greatest disaster of its kind in the history of the upper river—the barren sands were strewn with the bodies of innocent victims who, unlike Carl Getter, had committed no crime at all.

IO

THE LAST
STEAMBOAT

he Delaware River seems to have a dual personality split cleanly at Trenton Falls. Below Trenton the river is a deep, majestic thoroughfare, busy with ocean-going commerce—particularly around Philadelphia, a major seaport and a base for ships of the U.S. Navy. Above Trenton, the river is shallower, its raucous flow frequently inconvenienced by rapids and rifts. Before bridges were built, wagons could ford the upper river at certain points without the teamster risking wet feet, but at time of flood it could devastate the upper valley. The history of steamboat transportation on the Delaware River reflects this duality in an emphatic way.

The first steamboat in the United States (the invention of John Fitch) appeared in the waters of the lower Delaware in 1787. Steam vessels on the river above Trenton were much slower in coming. At various times in the first half of the nineteenth century, companies were formed and received franchises for steamboat routes on the upper river. One typical route involved was the *Major William Burnett*, a flat-bottomed steamer one hundred feet in length. This vessel carried freight and passengers between the Bel-Del railhead at Lambertville and Easton. The large craft had trouble negotiating rapids in this section of the river, especially in times of low water. It occasionally ran aground and often fell behind schedule. In the 1850s it was replaced by a smaller steamer called *Reindeer,* a sternwheeler. Before the end of the decade, this craft, too, had ceased operation, as had all other attempts along the upper river.

One final attempt was made to conquer the upper river by steam. In 1859 three leading citizens of Belvidere—Judge William Sharp, Richard Holcomb, and Alfred Thomas—formed the Kittatinny Improvement Company. Sharp and Thomas were prominent in both political and business circles in the county seat, and they had been instrumental in establishing the county's first fair and agricultural exposition at Belvidere. The articles of the Kittatinny Improvement Company stated that the purpose of the enterprise was to improve the river for steamboat traffic between Belvidere and Port Jervis, and, when this section of the river was deemed navigable even at low water, to operate a regular steamboat service between the two cities, a distance of some sixty miles. The corporation received a thirty-year monopoly on steamboat operation along this section of the Delaware with the obligation to "dredge, crib, riprap, and otherwise maintain the river in its area of operation." Their steamboats, however, could not interfere with the movement of other types of river craft such as timber rafts, Durham boats, and ferries.

On August 2, 1859, officers of the corporation and William Parks, a river expert, explored the upper Delaware in a Durham boat. Although the water level was at the year's low point, this group determined that with some expense the river here could be made navigable for steamboats, even in periods of extreme low water. Work began immediately, and the action was cheered by people living along the river. Land transportation was sketchy in the wilderness area through which the upper river flowed, and the isolated farmers there anticipated the coming of the steamboat with great enthusiasm.

While river improvements progressed, contracts were let for the construction of the steamer. Thomas Bishop of Easton was selected to build the hull. Bishop, considered one of the preeminent boat builders on the upper river, had achieved particular renown as a builder of Durham boats and canal boats. His boatyard stood on the north bank of the Lehigh River, a mere half mile from its juncture with the Delaware. Construction of the new steamship began immediately. A sternwheeler, the boat would have two decks, measure eighty-seven feet long and fifteen feet, 6 inches wide, and be of about seventy-five tons burden.

The two engines and the boiler were designed and built at the Wells Machine Shop in South Easton, under the supervision of engineer Samuel Shaeff of Easton. Shaeff, forty-five, would be chief engineer of the *Alfred Thomas* during its initial run up to Belvidere. His twenty-one-year-old son, George, would serve as his assistant and fireman.

By the first of the year, hull, engines, and boiler were completed and assembled. On January 16, 1860, the vessel—christened the *Alfred Thomas,* after one of the company's owners—received a trial run on the frigid waters of the Lehigh. Things did not go well during this trial—the steam engines seemed to be underpowered—and several changes were made: steam pipes to the engines were enlarged, oil spigots were installed on the steam chest to provide better lubrication for the piston rods, and an alteration was made to the steering mechanism. Also, a smoldering enmity that apparently existed between Bishop and Shaeff came to the surface during this run. Bishop warned Alfred Thomas that the boiler and engines were still "not right." Thomas then hired an engineer from Belvidere, who inspected the engines and boiler, recommended some minor adjustments, and, when they were completed, gave the craft a clean bill of health. This final approval was given on March 5. The boat would make her maiden voyage the next day.

On the morning of Tuesday, March 6, 1860, the *Alfred Thomas* steamed from Bishop's boatyard, destined for her home port in Belvidere. It would have to pass through some major rapids, especially the infamous Foul Rift, but spring freshet was at its peak and the depth of the river would help the ship get over the boulders and ledge rock. Also, negotiating these rapids would be a one-time ordeal. Once the craft reached Belvidere, it would operate upriver only and face just minor rifts.

With Old Glory flying from the upper deck and nearly a hundred passengers crowded aboard, the vessel steamed proudly down the Lehigh toward the Delaware. The day was springlike, and cheering crowds lined the river's banks. In anticipation of the coming Civil War, many felt that the steamer represented the naval and engineering superiority of the North, and this gave the occasion a patriotic flavor. Among those on board were the delighted owners, Sharp, Holcomb, and Thomas; Bishop and some of his employees; and Shaeff and his son, George, captain and crew.

Then as now, a dam spanned the Lehigh where it enters the larger river. Before reaching this obstruction, the boat exited the Lehigh via an outlock and entered the fast-flowing Delaware. At the outlock, the ever-skeptical Bishop insisted that he and his workers be put ashore. He explained later that he didn't feel the craft would perform well in the stronger current of the Delaware and he wanted to distance himself from an embarrassing failure.

Once on the Delaware, the craft proceeded upriver, struggling somewhat, but making progress with enough excess steam for an occasional blast of its whistle. The boat passed under the covered bridge that joined Phillipsburg with Easton, then turned toward the Pennsylvania bank. Here, it docked at a temporary pier at the foot of Spring Garden Street in front of Keller's Hotel, where most of the passengers ate lunch. When the boat started again for Belvidere, only thirty-two passengers were on board for this last leg of the journey. Among them were Holcomb, Thomas, and Judge Sharp, who was accompanied by his seventeen-year-old nephew, William.

Upriver from the pier at Kellers, near where Bushkill Creek enters the Delaware, Getter's Island occupies the very middle of the river. The long, low-lying island was named for Carl Getter, an itinerant laborer who had been hanged there thirty years before (see Chapter 9). Whether engineer Shaeff gave this incident any thought as he drew near the island, no one knows. We do know that spectators crowded the high banks on both sides of the river. The clearest transit around

Getter's Island in the Delaware. Here Carl Getter was hanged and the Alfred Thomas *exploded. (Photo courtesy of Ron Wynkoop Sr.)*

the island lay on the Jersey side, and soon the vessel was in this channel, laboring against the powerful current.

The *Alfred Thomas* had almost passed the island when it encountered rapids that, enhanced by the spring freshet, were more than the little craft could manage. The vessel hung here for some ten minutes, its steam pressure registering 60 pounds. Then Shaeff decided to let the craft drop down in the current and into an eddy near the island, where it could build up enough pressure to enable the steamer to force the rapids. When it reached the eddy, its bow was secured to a tree on the island to keep the craft from swinging into the current. Several passengers joined the younger Shaeff in cutting boards and throwing the pieces into the boiler's firebox, while others used poles to hold the craft to the shore. (Ironically, later testimony revealed that some passengers thought the *Alfred Thomas* had run aground and the men were trying to push the steamer *away* from the shore.) One passenger, Arthur Kessler, attempted to throw a rope to one of the small skiffs that had been launched from shore and now hovered around the *Alfred Thomas*. Peter Fisher, a friend of Sharp's and Thomas's who had urgent business in Belvidere, lost his patience with the delay and negotiated with one of the little skiffs to take him to the Jersey bank, where he could then proceed by train. Many excited passengers with apparently nothing to do ran from one side of the deck to the other, causing the vessel to rock and tilt ominously. Judge Sharp, the senior Shaeff, and another passenger, Joseph Losey, were grouped in front of the pressure gauges.

Soon, pressure in the boilers climbed to 125 pounds and somebody, a passenger apparently, rang the bell to start the paddle wheel turning.

The springlike temperatures that day caused many residents on both sides of the river to open their windows wide, and to them the explosion seemed especially loud. People from as far away as Belvidere and Washington claimed to have heard it. Some thought it was an earthquake; others suspected Confederate sabotage. Those spectators along the banks of the Delaware, however, had no doubt about what had happened: the *Alfred Thomas* had blown apart before their very eyes.

The steam boiler, located in the bow, had burst, and folks in that part of the craft—the engineer, those feeding the boiler's fires, and those grouped around the engines' gauges—died instantly. Samuel and George Shaeff were terribly mangled, the father's booted leg found in the wreckage days later. Both Judge Sharp and Richard Holcomb were killed, but some hope was held for the Judge's nephew, William, whose body could not be found. The third owner of the Kittatinny Improvement Company, Alfred Thomas, had been in the rear of the boat and escaped uninjured.

Many of the passengers were not as lucky as Thomas. George Smith, a twenty-five-year-old widower and father of two, was blown sixty feet to the shore of the island. His body was found face down in

The explosion of the Alfred Thomas *in the Delaware opposite Easton, Pennsylvania, on Tuesday, March 6, 1860. Sketch by J. Queen hangs in the Marx Room at the Easton Public Library. (Photo © by Diane A. Pratt)*

a few inches of water. The mutilated corpse of his friend, Joe Weaver, was found nearby. Two passengers, Robert Burrell and John Clifton, received slight injuries but still aided in the rescue work. They found lying in shallow water two other passengers, Sam Yates and Valentine Schooley, who both died soon after.

Several passengers were seen floating in the water, but before rescuers could reach them they disappeared. Witnesses saw one man—some thought it was young Sharp—blown high into the air; he landed in the main channel of the river and, before anyone could get to him, went under. Sharp and two prominent Eastonites, Stewart Beatty and Arthur Kessler, remained missing for several days, but eventually their bodies were recovered. Another Eastonite, Henry Metler, died of his wounds the first day.

Others were more fortunate. Edward McIntire, a leader in Easton's black community, was badly injured but survived. Eugene Troxell skyrocketed into the river but was hardly hurt at all. Peter Bercaw

broke his leg. Joseph Losey was found on the island completely dis-
oriented; he asked others what had happened, insisting he had not
been on the boat and had heard no explosion. Benjamin Youells
broke his leg in two places and received other injuries as well, but he
would survive well into the twentieth century, always willing to talk
about this experience. Robert Carhart, who had been going home to
Belvidere that day, survived uninjured; he, too, would spend the rest
of his life talking about this day to whomever would listen.

Charles Buck, another prominent Eastonite, had been lucky
enough to be on the stern of the boat when the blast occurred. He
told his story at the coroner's inquest:

> The first thing I knew after the explosion was the
> flying of fragments and someone crying, 'Mr. Buck,
> help me or I will die.' I cast my eyes forward and
> recognized Richard Williams who was pinned fast to
> the bench with a steam pipe laying across his neck
> and shoulders. I took a fragment of the wreck and
> pried the pipe up and relieved him and set him on
> the bench. I told him to set still but he jumped into
> the water. My attention was then directed to the Jer-
> sey side of the boat. Jumping down from the deck to
> the guard, I aided in getting Mr. Mellick from the
> water. I went below decks briefly and saw three per-
> sons lying in the cabin, all dead. I did not know
> them. On deck I saw five persons in the water with
> bloody faces, floating and struggling, and another
> floating on his back. I think he was Arthur Kessler. I
> remained on the wreck until it neared the bridge but
> recognized only Bercaw of those picked up.

Another survivor named Able reported at the inquest that a skiff
had rowed up to the shattered *Alfred Thomas*. While the skiff's owner
was pulling an exhausted man from the river, another passenger
jumped into the skiff from the railing and broke through the little
boat, sinking it. The man being saved, thought to be Beatty, lost his
grip and was carried away by the strong current.

According to Buck, the ravaged *Alfred Thomas,* its flag bravely flying, began to float downstream almost immediately after the explosion. It finally came to rest against a pier of the railroad bridge, where it remained for several days until it was towed back to Bishop's boatyard.

Soon after the calamity, crowds of people rushed to Getter's Island—among them several physicians, who set up a first-aid station and treated the injured. Several bodies were taken to the old courthouse in Center Square, then later removed to their homes. Curiosity seekers collected pieces of the hull and boiler—as well as more gruesome objects. Someone found Holcomb's gold watch, cut from its chain and blown to the island.

The next day, the coroner of Northampton County called a jury to investigate the accident and to determine its cause. That afternoon, the jury examined the bodies and the wreckage, and the following day began to hear testimony.

Survivors, including Buck, Able, Burrell, and Alfred Thomas, told their stories. Thomas, who had also been involved in the design and construction of the craft, testified to some of the problems in the trial run but said he believed they had been corrected.

Bishop, the hull builder, was vehement in his criticism of the dead engineer. He told the jury that he had informed the owners of Shaeff's incompetence and warned them that the engines and boiler were not performing properly, but that their only response had been, "We'll try it and see."

Several steam engineers, former railroaders mostly, asserted that the boiler had not been strong enough to withstand the pressures involved and that the gauges had been installed incorrectly and, hence, could not accurately record the steam pressure.

Finally, an expert witness, Doctor T. Green, testified that as the boat pulled away from the island, just prior to the catastrophe, cold water from the river was pumped into the overheated boiler. He said this condition would create steam pressure of 750 pounds per square inch and "exert the force of gunpowder."

All of the testimony, whether pertaining to the design and construction of the boiler or the operation of the engines, incriminated

Samuel Shaeff, who could not defend himself. Nor could any refutation be offered by the other dead crew member, his son.

The final rebuke came a short time later when the much respected *Scientific American* reviewed the testimony and other evidence, and concluded: "There is no mystery as to the cause of this explosion; the boiler was managed as with an intent to commit suicide."

Though at the hearing Samuel Shaeff was blamed for the disaster, it eventually came to be realized that the real malefactor was the river itself. Never again would commercial steamboat travel be attempted on the upper river.

The *Alfred Thomas,* however, lived on. Thomas Bishop rebuilt the hull; new engines and a new boiler were installed, and the craft was converted to a ferry and exiled to a remote crossing on the Schuylkill River. When the Peninsular Campaign of the Civil War got underway, the steamer was called to active duty running supplies up the James River to Union troops pinned down near Richmond. Thus, the indomitable *Alfred Thomas* had a taste of glory, after all.

II

THE PEA PATCH

ea Patch Island. The earliest maps of the Delaware River didn't show it at all. Then, according to legend, an errant skiffload of peas overturned on a sandbar and took root. Around this nucleus the island grew. By the end of the eighteenth century, mapmakers had found it.

Positioned where the river narrows just above the bay, Pea Patch Island commands much of the river's width. As early as 1814, military leaders recommended it as a site for a fortification to protect the bountiful river valley and the upriver cities of Wilmington and Philadelphia. Unfortunately, at high tide the island almost completely disappeared underwater. This difficulty could be overcome, the engineers calculated, by the construction of a levee around the entire island. The levee was built, as was the fort; completed in 1859, it was named Fort Delaware. During the Civil War, the United States government decided to imprison here Confederate soldiers who were unfortunate enough to be captured.

The fate of these Confederate captives was for years one of the best kept secrets of the war. Conditions at Southern prisoner-of-war compounds became well known due to post-war trials of commandants and the lurid and shocking tales told by returned Yankee prisoners. Not until this century, however, with the formation of the

Fort Delaware Society, did the truth about conditions at this Northern prison become common knowledge. The society was founded in 1950 by private citizens to preserve and research the fort, which had been closed as a military post a few years earlier. Membership consisted mainly of residents of nearby states whose sympathies were as mixed as their forebears' had been. Since then, the society has published a number of diaries, journals, and letters, as well as its own bulletin, *Fort Delaware Notes,* that tell of a side to the prison long unknown.

Early in the Civil War, being captured was a temporary inconvenience. By unwritten agreement, the two sides exchanged captives promptly, and prisoner-of-war camps such as Fort Delaware were mere holding pens containing a few hundred prisoners. As black units of the Northern army entered into action, however, the agreement collapsed. President Jefferson Davis refused to exchange black captives, claiming they were runaway slaves and, as such, belonged to Confederate citizens. General Halleck, Lincoln's chief of staff, retaliated by cancelling all prisoner exchanges. Principle aside, Northern generals agreed that Lee's dwindling forces were benefitting inordinately from the transfusion of recycled soldiery. They felt, too, that the need to feed thousands of Yankee captives would put an unbearable strain on the South's already overtaxed food production. By May 1863 most prisoner exchanges had ceased.

This had unexpected consequences for some prisoners in a group that escaped before it even got to the fort. In June 1863 about a hundred prisoners who were being brought to Fort Delaware aboard the steamer *Maple Leaf* seized control of the ship as it neared Chesapeake Bay. Under the leadership of a Confederate naval captain, Emelious Fuller, they made it to shore in friendly territory. Oddly, some of the prisoners chose not to escape. A few were too sick for the attempt, but others expected to be exchanged when they reached Fort Delaware and felt they would get home soon anyway, legitimately. But at about this time the exchange of prisoners ceased and they had to wait until the end of the war to get home—if they survived.

"Fresh fish"—new prisoners arriving at Fort Delaware. (Photo courtesy of the Fort Delaware Society)

Captured troops began to accumulate in large numbers on both sides. In May 1863, for example, 1,255 men were confined at Fort Delaware; by July, after the Battle of Gettysburg, the prisoner population at the fort had increased more than ten-fold, to 12,595.

To accommodate this huge influx of soldiers, wooden barracks were hastily thrown up outside the bastion's walls, on the north side of the island. Henceforth, only high-ranking Confederate officers and a few civilians were held within the fort itself. The new barracks stood on a five-acre marsh crisscrossed by drainage canals. Latrines were built out over the river, but the canals themselves were used for bathing, washing clothes, even for fishing. It was thought, erroneously, that the ebb and flow of the tides would keep the canals flushed clean.

In this flimsy and crowded housing, thousands of prisoners fell victim to malaria, dysentery, typhoid, and malnutrition. Most of the

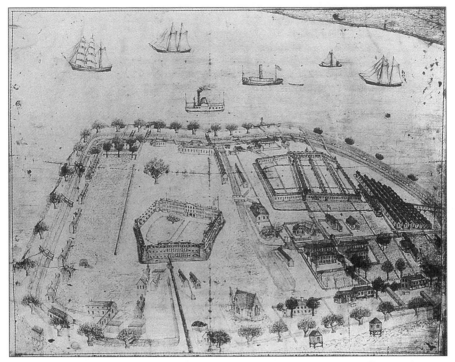

A prisoner made this drawing of the island. High-ranking Confederate officers and civilian prisoners were held in the fort itself (the five-sided structure in the center). All other prisoners were housed in wooden barracks to the right and rear of the fort. (Photo courtesy of the Fort Delaware Society)

seriously ill were jammed into the hospital, but many refused hospitalization, fearing the contagion there. Hundreds died, but even in death their bodies found no peace; incoming tides pushed them up from their island graves. Authorities then decided to rebury the dead on the mainland, at nearby Finns Point, New Jersey. By the end of the war, more than twenty-four hundred Confederate bodies had been dumped there in a communal grave.

One prisoner who seemed destined for the Finns Point cemetery was Sam W. Paulette. Paulette had arrived at the fort with the large contingent of Gettysburg captives on July 7, 1863. The nineteen-year

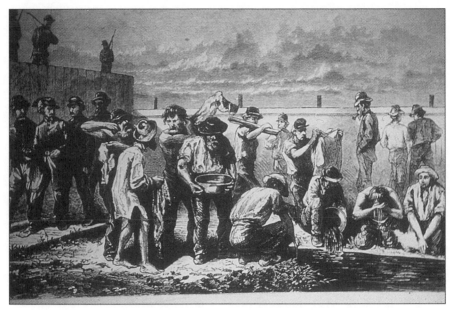

The canals around the barracks served for bathing, washing clothes, and fishing. It was calculated, mistakenly, that tidal action would flush out the canals.
(Photo courtesy of the Fort Delaware Society)

old private stood five feet, six inches tall but weighed only ninety pounds, more the result of metabolism than lack of food. His friends in the eighteenth Virginia swore that a bullet could never hit him as long as he stood sideways to the enemy.

Young Sam volunteered to carry lumber from a ship at dockside to the barracks under construction. In compensation, he would receive an extra meal each day. The sight of the scrawny boy staggering under a load of lumber touched the sergeant-of-the-guard, who decided to let Paulette supervise the unloading. The vessel, the *Osceola,* also carried passengers, and they, too, took pity on the wretched-looking captive. Paulette was soon doing a thriving business selling these people rings and carvings made by his fellow prisoners. The money he earned enabled him to buy from crew members extra food that was far superior to the meager prison fare.

Prison barracks on the swampy northern end of the island. (Photo courtesy of the Fort Delaware Society)

The food shortage that developed in the last half of 1863 was never overcome. Indeed, when word of conditions at the Confederate prison in Andersonville, Georgia, reached the North early in 1864, many Yankee jailers took it upon themselves to retaliate by cutting the rations of the rebels even further.

Samuel Hardinge, a United States naval officer who had deserted to marry the notorious Confederate spy, Belle Boyd, kept a diary while imprisoned at Fort Delaware. "Two meals were served to us," he wrote, "consisting of one piece of peculiarly constructed bread and one *ditto* of indescribable salt, yellowish colored, pork that had the nutriment boiled out of it."

Randolph Shotwell, a prisoner from North Carolina, confirmed this menu but added that rice soup was served occasionally. "It was a standing joke," he wrote, "that this soup was too weak to *drown* the rice worms and pea bugs, which, however, came to their death by *starvation.*"

Shotwell gave this picture of imprisoned officers attempting to supplement their meat ration: "It is a curious sight to see grown men, whiskered and uniformed officers who have already 'set a squadron in the field,' lurking, club in hand, near one of the many breathing holes which the long-tailed rodents have dug in the hard earth, patiently awaiting a chance to strike a blow 'for fresh meat and rat soup' for dinner. They generally succeed."

Soon, scurvy joined the list of prisoner afflictions. Captain Robert Park of the twelfth Alabama wrote: "The poor fellows suffering from scurvy are a sad sight. Their legs and feet are so drawn up as to compel them to walk on tiptoe, their heels being unable to touch the floor as they walk from their beds to huddle around the stove."

Winters were especially difficult for the Southerners. Each building held four hundred men and had two coal-burning stoves. A prisoner was allowed only one blanket and little extra clothing. Those who arrived on the island with more than this were forced to surrender all additional items to the guards. Some men got the use of an extra blanket by sleeping in shifts with a comrade; one slept during the day under two blankets while his partner huddled around the stove or went out on a work detail. At night they switched places.

Prisoner W. H. Moon of Goldwater, Alabama, told of another problem: "The barracks being very open, in cold weather the heat could be felt but a short distance even from a red-hot stove. . . . Those who crowded around the stove continually were dubbed 'stove rats.' On very cold days those who spent most of their time on their bunks trying to keep warm would get down in the passage between the bunks and charge the 'stove rats' and take their turn at the stove."

Smallpox struck in the fall of 1863. Approximately 15 percent of the prisoners fell ill from this disease and about half of the afflicted died. Attempts to transfer some prisoners to alleviate the unhealthy overcrowding failed, since the commandants of other camps feared the spread of the disease to their prisoners.

During the 1863–1864 winter, burial details were overwhelmed. Some guards and prisoners did nothing but dig graves, and even then bodies piled up, unburied, at Finns Point. The death rate at Fort

Delaware for October 1863 was 12 1/2 percent of the prison population, the highest of any prisoner-of-war compound, North or South.
When the Confederate exchange commissioner, Robert Ould, complained to Lincoln's secretary of war, Edwin Stanton, that the North
was killing prisoners by deliberate mistreatment, Stanton denied the
charge and had the surgeon general investigate. The surgeon general
reported that prison conditions in the North were, indeed, appalling,
that the death rate was a disgrace, and that some prisoners should
be transferred at once to relieve the overcrowding. His report was
ignored.

The camp commander at Fort Delaware from 1863 to the end of
the war was Brigadier General Albin F. Schoepf, a Hungarian by birth
and a failed combat leader. The aristocratic Schoepf fully enjoyed the
privileges of rank and delighted in associating with high-ranking
military and political prisoners. He had little direct contact with
field-grade officers and enlisted men. Schoepf left the day-to-day operation of the prison to his adjutant, Captain George Ahl, who was
vigorously assisted by Lieutenant Abraham Wolf. The prisoners de-
spised both men and felt that complaints addressed to Schoepf were
pigeonholed by these subordinates. Randolph Shotwell, who had a
way with words, referred to Ahl as "an autocratic Bashaw of ten tails,
who is, all in Ahl, Ahl-fired mean."

Wolf, a former sergeant, had risen through the ranks of the guards.
The tall, mustached Pennsylvanian was a martinet who enjoyed his
life-and-death authority over the prisoners. He established among the
captives a network of spies and informers who, for extra food and
privileges, kept him apprised of any undercover activities. Several escape attempts were frustrated in this way. Wolf conducted frequent
surprise searches of the barracks and confiscated any contraband, as
well as extra clothing, blankets, and food. The men called him the
Fox or Spaniel for his ability to sniff out any breach of regulations.
Sam Paulette called Wolf "the meanest Yankee I ever saw," and became furious when Wolf addressed him as "boy." "Lieutenant," he
said, "you can call me what you want here, but I want you to know I
fill a man's shoes in Dixie."

The guards at Fort Delaware were, for the most part, militia or one-hundred-day men, all non-combatants. One of them, Private A. J. Hamilton, kept a journal in which he described drunkenness, thievery, and brawling among his fellow soldiers as well as the officers. He told of the guards firing their weapons indiscriminately and accidentally killing prisoners (as well as, on one occasion, another guard). Hamilton referred to the prisoners as "miserable, filthy, rascals" and "vile wretches." He wrote, "I am amused at the Johnnies snatching and grabbing for the slops from the cookhouse."

Those prisoners strong enough for the dangerous swim to the mainland frequently tried to escape, gaining undetected access to the river through the privy holes. In the summer of 1863, six prisoners escaped with improvised life preservers made from empty, well-corked canteens. Some of them were swept sixteen miles downriver. Still, all but one made it to the Delaware shore, where local farmers gave them food and shelter. Rebel sentiment ran so strong in Delaware and Maryland that escapees had a good chance at freedom once they got off the island. The escapees finally rejoined Lee's army in Virginia. Later in the year, two hundred men fled from Fort Delaware in a single night. Area residents in boats picked up many of this group and helped them on their way.

One enterprising prisoner hid in a coffin and was taken with several corpses to the Finns Point cemetery. As he was being lowered into a trench, he burst out of the pine box and disappeared into the woods. In the confusion, several prisoners in the burial detail also got away. Apparently, none were recaptured.

Of the prisoners at Fort Delaware, only the strongest both physically and psychologically survived. They attempted to adjust to their situation and to carry on something approximating a normal existence. Some became barbers, others did shoe repair or cleaned laundry. Some even made and sold rings and other trinkets as souvenirs to guards and visitors. The money or goods these men earned enabled them to buy food, tobacco, and other amenities from the underground commerce of the prison, thus increasing their chances of survival.

Lieutenant Tom Jones of North Carolina learned how to brew beer from hardtack. He sold the beverage to guards and anyone else who could afford it. When he gained his freedom after the war, he went home with several hundred dollars in U.S. currency. With this capital he founded a carriage manufacturing business in Carthage, North Carolina, and ultimately retired a rich and respected member of the community.

The ubiquitous Sam Paulette used some of his *Osceola* earnings to buy a hook and line from one of the guards. He fished at a spot where camp cooks dumped garbage into the river; there he caught enough catfish to feast like a gourmand and have a large surplus as well. He sold all this excess and soon joined the ranks of prison capitalists.

The more intellectual of the incarcerated held classes in foreign and classical languages, mathematics, law, and literature. One prisoner gave guitar lessons. Debating societies, Bible study groups, and a chorus were formed, as was a newspaper. Captain J. W. Hibbs, a Richmond journalist before the war, published the *Prison Times*. The first and only issue came out near the end of the war, in April 1865. It was hand-written, with a large staff of prisoners making copies. The paper contained two pages of ads by inmates who offered their services as tailors, dentists, tobacconists, cobblers, and more. It reported on chess tournaments and concerts, and noted the efforts of a Prisoner Benevolent Association that worked in behalf of sick or destitute men. Two "butchers" advertised rat meat for sale, indicating that even at war's end prison rations remained inadequate.

Escape and death were not the only routes out of captivity, though. A few sick men were exchanged. (Wraithlike Sam Paulette was sent home to Farmville, Virginia, in 1864, ostensibly to die.) And the Federal Government offered a pardon to any Confederate who would take the oath of allegiance. Captain Ahl and Lieutenant Wolf put intense pressure on prisoners to accept the offer, but few succumbed. Those who took the oath at this time were held in great contempt by their fellow prisoners and were labeled "galvanized" or "whitewashed" Yankees. And, much to their chagrin, they were not given their freedom as promised. Instead, they remained on the island as hospital orderlies or guards. In one instance, some two hundred prisoners joined the U.S. Army under the impression that they would be sent west to fight American Indians. They were formed into the first Delaware Heavy Artillery with Ahl and Wolf as commander and adjutant, respectively. The unit never left the island.

Those who "took the yellow dog," as it was called, received better food and quarters, and some undoubtedly kept alive in this way. Sadly, they were considered traitors by the majority, and many never returned to their homes in the South.

Lee's surrender at Appomattox on April 9, 1865, changed everything. Many of the prisoners, especially those who had served under Lee, now took the oath and were released. When General Joseph E. Johnston surrendered in North Carolina a few weeks later, the oath was offered again and a large group of prisoners took it and went free.

At this time, final word of the indomitable Paulette reached his comrades on the island. He'd rejoined his old regiment, the Eighteenth Virginia, and fought in its ranks throughout the bloody Wilderness campaign. Then, only three days before Lee's surrender, he was badly wounded and recaptured at Saylor's Creek, just a few miles from his home. He survived his wounds and, at war's end, was sent home for good. He had, indeed, "filled a man's shoes in Dixie."

Still, thousands of prisoners who refused to take the oath remained on the island. This decision cost many their lives; some two hundred men died here after Lee's surrender. Finally, on June 27, the holdouts were freed by order of General Grant—without having to take the yellow dog.

After the war, the fort fell dormant; only a small caretaker detachment remained. In 1896, a major modernization of the fort's armament was carried out and completed in time for the Spanish-American War, when the U.S. government considered the Spanish fleet in Cuba a threat. But the fort saw no action in this war nor in the two world wars. In 1945 the government declared the fort surplus property. Its guns had never fired a shot in anger.

Monument at Finns Point, New Jersey, marks the mass grave of over twenty-four hundred Confederates who died while captives at Fort Delaware. (Photo by Diana Dale)

Fort Delaware has been named a National Historic Site for its role in the Civil War. More recently, the State of Delaware has turned it into a state park and provides regular ferry service to the island, except in the winter months. From the ramparts of the bastion one can see the obelisk on the Jersey shore that marks the mass grave at Finns Point National Cemetery, reminder of a most shameful episode on an island in the Delaware River called Pea Patch.

12

MANUNKA CHUNK HOUSE

ignificant things happened 120 years ago in the village of Manunka Chunk, on the shores of the upper Delaware. Two major railroads—the Delaware, Lackawanna & Western, from Hoboken, and the Pennsylvania, from Philadelphia—decided to form a junction here. Both built and shared new freight and passenger stations, rail yards, and a tower, and thus could transfer to each others' lines at will. By this cooperative venture, completed in 1876, each railroad greatly increased the service it could offer its customers without having to build new trackage and bridges. Manunka Chunk became a major rail center that few other towns in western New Jersey could match.

For years both railroads had been bringing vacationers from the Newark and Philadelphia areas to the fine hotels located at the Delaware Water Gap, a few miles north of Manunka Chunk. Well-to-do families from towns such as Montclair, Bryn Mawr, Paoli, and Morristown came here on the trains for the cooling breezes, refreshing waters, and outstanding scenery of the upper Delaware. At first, Manunka Chunk had little to entice these summer visitors, but the construction of the rail junction offered entrepreneurial possibilities too obvious to ignore.

Fred Dopke had been a New York City policeman who received his baptism of fire in the bloody Civil War draft riots in that city. He came to western New Jersey for a better, less violent life, sensed the potential for a fine hotel, and in 1885 purchased an island across from Manunka Chunk on which to build the place. The island, a Lenni-Lenape campsite in bygone years, has over the years been known by many names—Macks, Manunka Chunk, Dildines, Brisbanes—but as long as Fred Dopke and family owned it, it was called, fittingly enough, Dopke's Island. Eighty-five acres in size, it had high banks and a fine sandy beach on its lower end. Dopke's Hotel was built in 1886 and opened its doors for business in the summer of that year. The imposing structure immediately became a landmark on the river for those who canoed or fished, and especially for the timber raftsmen who rushed by on spring freshet, riding their humpbacked cargo to mills downriver.

Dopke or his son, Henry, met arriving guests at the Manunka Chunk station and took them by buggy to the riverbank opposite the island. The stream here was usually shallow—the main channel lay on the Pennsylvania side of the island—and the horse-drawn vehicle simply forded the river to the hotel. If the water level was too high for this, Dopke kept a ferry that could carry guests, luggage, and even the horse and buggy to the island, all in fine style.

First-time visitors were struck by the grandeur of the hostelry. A three-story frame structure, it contained sixty-five sleeping rooms and had piazzas on the first two levels that wrapped around the building on three sides. The first floor had a music room with piano (one of Dopke's daughters was an excellent pianist), a ballroom, a billiard room, a parlor where books and games could be enjoyed, and, of course, a large dining room. Local women, used to preparing hearty meals for farmer-husbands, were hired to do the cooking at the hotel,

Manunka Chunk Station, which served both the Pennsylvania Railroad and the Delaware, Lackawanna, and Western Railroad. (Photo from author's collection)

which soon became famous for the quantity of its cuisine. The Dopkes maintained a farm on the island and could offer fresh vegetables and eggs each day. Fine melons were grown in season on the island's sandy lower end, and the hotel's cows kept the ice boxes filled with milk and butter. Near the hotel, Dopke built an ice house in which he stored ice cut from the river and packed in sawdust. Here meat was kept fresh and ice maintained for drinks sipped on the piazza on hot summer days.

Guests could swim, fish, or boat "away from noise, dust and mosquitos," according to ads in Newark newspapers, or play tennis on the hotel's courts. Many folks, however, preferred strolling on the piazza or reclining in one of the hammocks stretched between shade trees in the grove at water's edge; for exhausted Wall Street executives, this was activity enough. By the time of Fred Dopke's death in 1895, the place had a reputation as one of the outstanding establish-

The hotel ferry taking guests to the island. (Photo from author's collection)

ments in the Delaware Valley and rarely had an empty room during its Memorial Day–to–Labor Day season. Henry Dopke took over the operation on his father's death and, with his wife and children, moved from Belvidere to live on the island year round. After the hotel closed for the season, Henry took produce from the farm into Belvidere to sell. The melons were especially favored by local residents.

The hotel flourished for eight years under Henry Dopke's management, until the Pumpkin Freshet of October 1903 (see chapter 13). Nine inches of rain fell in thirty hours, creating the worst deluge, up to that time, in the recorded history of the river. Nine of the Delaware's wooden bridges, including Belvidere's covered span, were swept away. Dopke's Island had never before been completely swamped; this time the water rose halfway to the second floor of the hotel. After freeing the farm animals, Dopke loaded his family and belongings on the ferry and just barely made it through raging waters to the mainland. Heartbroken, he never returned to his beloved hotel.

The place sat idle until 1905, when it was purchased by Mrs. M. L. Brisbane. She renovated it and, for a time, the hotel, now rechristened the Manunka Chunk House, regained some of the grandeur of

Guests at the hotel on Dopke's Island, circa 1890. Note first and second floor piazzas.
The hotel's name later became Manunka Chunk House.
(From private collection of William Dopke)

former years. After World War I the Red Cross leased the hotel for a year as a place for wounded soldiers suffering mostly from shell shock, to recuperate. (Area residents, however, were sometimes disconcerted to meet an obviously disturbed patient walking on a lonely country road.) In 1920 guests returned on a regular basis and shared the island with football teams from Easton's Lafayette College. The teams held summer practice on the island but stayed at a less expensive boarding house on the Jersey mainland. The undefeated team of 1921, coached by the legendary Jock Sutherland, honed its skills here, and guests were thrilled to have this opportunity to watch these local heroes in action.

In 1925 Frank Ransom, son of Mrs. Brisbane, took over management and ownership of Manunka Chunk House and had as a business partner a Mrs. Ruthinger, whom he later married. Ransom erected a large metal sign with the hotel's name on it easily visible

Manunka Chunk House, circa 1920s. (Photo courtesy of Richard Ransom)

from Route 6 (now Route 46) in New Jersey. A brochure put out by the new owners gave directions for automobile routes to the hotel, the railroad station having been abandoned at Manunka Chunk after a washout in 1913. The brochure touted the "generous table of whole-some, well-cooked food, milk, and fresh vegetables," as well as the presence of a radio in the parlor. Rates, including meals, were twenty dollars a week or four dollars a day.

The ferry to the island was no longer in use but, if necessary, guests could be taken across the river in one of the many rowboats on hand. A Model-T Ford, driven over to the island at low water, pro-vided visitors with a vehicle for sightseeing excursions around the grounds. Guests also enjoyed searching for Indian relics, with which the fields abounded.

But none of these things could counteract the stock market crash of 1929 and the Depression that followed. People were more con-cerned with going to work than going on vacation, and the fortunes of Manunka Chunk House declined precipitously in the early 1930s. By 1935, Ransom could no longer keep up the mortgage payments and ownership of the hotel reverted to the mortgage holder, Celia Emery of Mount Bethel, Pennsylvania. She held a sale shortly after taking over in an attempt to recoup some of her losses. Local residents, many of whom were visiting the hotel for the first and last time, still remember the sale today. Among the most memorable sites were the pool table and piano being rowed across the river, each on a pair of rowboats lashed side-by-side, and the Model-T being negotiated across the river by its new owner. Soon, the abandoned hotel fell into disuse.

Midday on June 13, 1938, a local resident, Mabel Smith, was working in her garden on the Pennsylvania riverbank opposite the island. She looked up to see a puff of smoke appear above the trees and she knew immediately what had happened. Around the same time, Belvidere firefighters arrived on the Jersey side of the river. With no way to get their equipment out to the island, they could only watch as the old hotel, and the farmhouse next to it, went up in flames. Arson was suspected but never proved.

After the fire, Emery sold off plots on the island to a few vacationers, who built cottages at the river's edge and continued to enjoy the island's beauty. The island was again devastated by flooding in August 1955 when Hurricane Diane hit the area. But the Belvidere Rescue Squad managed to rescue those staying on the island, and not a life was lost.

In the 1970s, the State of New Jersey became interested in the island for part of its parks and recreation program. In 1979, with the help of Green Acres funds, the island was purchased and is now administered by the state. Present plans call for the establishment of a canoe camping area here, offering to the canoeist a high, dry campsite for the night and a fine beach to relax on for a few hours—amenities enjoyed by only a select few in the past. Maybe the best days for the island are just ahead.

13

THE
PUMPKIN
FRESHET
OF 1903

ost people in the Delaware Valley welcomed the freshets that happened every spring and often in the fall. The result of snowmelt and seasonal rain, a freshet added enough water to the river to carry timber rafts and other craft through the rapids and over the falls to markets downstream. Without a freshet, the river above Trenton would have little commercial value; Skinners Falls, Wells Falls, and Foul Rift would render it impassable.

But the valley's early residents, with their penchant for understatement, applied the same word to the bridge-smashing, house-floating, killing floods that nature inflicted on the river every generation or so. In the Bridges Freshet of January 1841, ice-choked flood waters reduced to kindling nine bridges spanning the river and swept away farms, ferries, and riverside hamlets. The Bridges Freshet, because of its vast destruction and the astounding thirty-five-foot flood level recorded at Easton, became the landmark deluge in the Delaware Valley by which all others would be judged—until the Halloween surprise of October 1903, called, appropriately, the Pumpkin Freshet.

Newspapers for the mid-Atlantic states predicted, with blissful but unwarranted optimism, that on Thursday, October 8, 1903, the region would get some rain and then the skies would clear. They were half right. It *did* rain but the skies didn't clear—not until the following Monday. On Thursday in North Jersey, 9.4 inches of rain fell. On Friday morning, between eight and ten o'clock alone, an astounding 2.42 inches fell. Horses drowned on the streets of Brooklyn; the dam at Pompton Lake collapsed; downtown Paterson was flooded to a depth of 10 feet. Bridges crowded with people watching the flood were swept away; New York City subways and Scranton coal mines filled with water. Rail, canal, and highway transportation ceased.

In the Delaware Valley, residents had to deal not only with the rain, but with water rushing downriver from the Pocono and Catskill watersheds. As one local farmer put it, "We thought Thursday was bad until Friday came along." By Thursday night the Delaware at Easton had risen to the level of the Lehigh River dam, which meant that the Lehigh's water would back up into the city. And warnings came from Port Jervis that worse was on the way.

The true dimensions of the flood became obvious when its crest hit Flatbrookville on the Warren County border. The water level of the river registered ten feet above the record set by the great flood of 1841. At Portland, Main Street lay under five feet of water. At Manunka Chunk, just downriver, pumpkins growing among the cornstalks on the bottom land were swept away. They were identified in the morning light and, as more appeared in the river, the freshet got its name. Few people were aware that an October flood in 1786 and another in 1869 were similarly named. In Manunka Chunk a band of Gypsies searched for high ground and found it just in time. The fine hotel on Dopke's Island, closed for the winter, had muddy river water lapping at its second-floor balcony. Near Phillipsburg a farmer was wading

View of Water Street, Person's Corner, Belvidere, New Jersey, looking east from bridge.
(Photo courtesy of private collection of Betty Jo King, Washington, New Jersey)

in his barnyard, attempting to save his animals, when he turned to see his house move off its foundation. He chased the floating building—his family was still inside—and finally boarded the roof. Downriver a party of rescuers removed the farmer and another man who had gotten on board. They tore off shingles to get to the attic, where the farmer's wife and two children were huddled. All were saved.

The bridge between Port Jervis and Matamoras, a 651-foot landmark, was one of the first to be destroyed by the flood's crest. Several people who were on it drowned. Pieces of bridges, timber rafts torn from their moorings, uprooted trees, and buildings smashed into the mostly wooden bridges downstream. The sturdy covered bridge between Portland and Columbia miraculously held, but downriver at Belvidere it was a different story. There the span crossing to Riverton, a fine covered bridge built in 1839, was supposed to be flood-proof. After an all-day buffeting by the flotsam of trees, outhouses,

Bridge at Belvidere, New Jersey, a typical wooden covered bridge of the time. Note two openings and chutes along the side of bridge; workers would shovel horse manure down the chutes into the river. This bridge was destroyed in the flood of 1903. (Photo courtesy of private collection of Betty Jo King, Washington, New Jersey)

and timber rafts, however, the sixty-four-year old structure gave way. The Jersey end went first, followed by the Pennsylvania section.

The next bridge downstream was the Martins Creek structure, a long wooden trestle built for the Bangor and Portland Railroad. Workers at the Alpha Cement plant in Pennsylvania used the bridge to walk back and forth from their homes in Brainards. Train crews pushed a half-dozen wooden boxcars onto it to hold it in place, but to no avail. The span broke into sections that floated in the torrent toward Phillipsburg, the boxcars bobbing along behind.

The Phillipsburg-Easton bridge, a steel cantilever structure built only eight years before, had been designed by Professor J. Madison Porter, who also supervised its construction. Porter claimed his unique cantilever design made the bridge virtually indestructible. The professor, an Easton resident, was present now, his reputation on the line. The *Easton Express* reported, "Great crowds were at the bridge

View from Front Street in Belvidere, west of the Pennsylvania Railroad bridge, during the flood of 1903. (Photo courtesy of private collection of Betty Jo King, Washington, New Jersey)

watching the water creeping over the piers and carrying buildings, rafts, and other timber into the structure." Several shanties, thought to be homes of "Italians at Martin's Creek," struck the bridge; they were crushed like eggshells and passed under the structure. Then three rafts of heavy logs, torn loose from their moorings at Eddyside, "struck the bridge with tremendous force; two were forced under the bridge by the current, the third lodged near the western shore." When pieces of the Martins Creek railroad bridge struck the steel span, they, too, either shattered or passed under the deck, and the floating boxcars were reduced to splinters. Some of this debris continued downriver and caused some damage to the nearby Central Railroad bridge, but a string of loaded coal cars atop this span held it in place. Professor Porter's creation survived with flying colors; the local press dubbed it the "Gibraltar of the Delaware." Other bridges downstream at Riegelsville, Milford, Frenchtown, and Trenton were not so fortunate; all were swept away.

A house at the corner of Wall and Water streets, Belvidere, New Jersey. Water is just entering first-floor windows. (Photo courtesy of private collection of Betty Jo King, Washington, New Jersey)

All of the villages and cities along the river were badly damaged. In Belvidere, where the flooded Pequest joined the overflowing Delaware, the water submerged Depue, Water, Front, and even fashionable Greenwich streets; some homes had water to the second floor. Homeowners got some of their furniture to higher, drier levels, but frequently the most prized piece, the heavy parlor piano, was abandoned to the elements. Boardman's icehouse on the Pequest was carried into the Delaware along with one hundred tons of ice.

Easton, built where the Lehigh and Bushkill rivers join the Delaware, also was hard hit. The city lost hotels, trolleys, gas and electric plants, and its sewer plant, as well as most businesses. Homes along the Lehigh, Bushkill, and Delaware rivers lay underwater; The Mineral Springs and Sandts Eddy hotels were swamped. Phillipsburg received similar devastation. A railroad center, the city was put out of business; its industrial area, situated along the river, lay under six

The Columbia-Portland covered bridge survived the Pumpkin Flood of 1903.
(From private collection of William Dopke)

more feet of water than it had in the 1841 flood. The city's main industry, Andover Iron Company, was located between the railroad tracks and the river; it was almost completely submerged. Of the workers' homes nearby, the *Easton Express* reported: "the houses on this street, occupied by the foreign element, were half hidden by the water, the foreigners moved their household effects to the garrets."

Dairy farming, a major agricultural activity in the valley, came to a standstill. Creameries could not ship their milk because the railroads weren't functioning. So, to prevent spoilage, the dairy farmers made butter and cheese until the trains began moving again.

The water stopped rising by Saturday night, and by Sunday the water levels were receding. The area's greatest flood had ended. The death tolls in New Jersey and New York were high; even ships off the Jersey coast had been sunk with great loss of life. Most of the deaths in the Delaware Valley had come to people standing on bridges that were washed away. At Manunka Chunk two bodies were found together in a melon field. They were identified as men who had looked for shelter at the Gypsy camp but had been sent on their way. Apparently, they had taken refuge Saturday night in a shed in the field, and when the water rose they had been trapped. The Gypsies recalled hearing someone calling for help but had been powerless to respond. A valise containing burglar's tools was found near the bodies. The strangers, according to local papers, "appeared to be Germans" but were never identified.

Only two pedestrian bridges remained along the entire length of the river; the Phillipsburg-Easton cantilever and the old covered bridge between Columbia and Portland. It would be years before the others could be replaced. Ferries, long abandoned, were put back into operation, but travelers never got used to the inconvenience—or to the danger of collisions with timber rafts. At Brainards, the Alpha Cement Company put the naptha launch *Nellie* into operation. Captained by Joe Zelner, it carried workers to their jobs on the Pennsylvania shore. A good thing, too, for the bridge there was not rebuilt until 1907.

And Halloween was spoiled for the kids that year—there wasn't an outhouse left to be tipped.

14

THE LIFE
AND TIMES
OF BRAINARDS

ement—or its nearly perfect refinement, portland cement—was the miracle construction material of the early twentieth century. Portland cement was the essential ingredient of concrete, which came into its own just in time for the major construction projects of the Delaware, Lackawanna & Western Railroad. These projects—one in New Jersey, one in Pennsylvania—were called the cut-offs, and they included four concrete bridges: two in Pennsylvania, one in New Jersey, and one that crossed the Delaware between the two states. Each, when built, was the largest of its kind in the world. (The huge railroad bridge at Nicholson, Pennsylvania, still a breathtaking sight, was called the "Eighth Wonder of the World.") Along the cut-offs, even the stations and tunnels were poured from concrete. By the time World War I exploded, technology had advanced to the point where ships made of concrete were being constructed at the Hog Island Shipyard in the Delaware River below Philadelphia.

The Alpha cement plant in Martins Creek, Pennsylvania, where the Brainards men went to work, circa 1906. Note the limestone quarry at left.
(Photo courtesy of Ron Wynkoop Sr.)

Thomas Edison, who knew a good thing when he saw it, had built a cement plant in 1901 at New Village in Warren County, New Jersey. (Edison used limestone from his quarry in nearby Oxford.) By the 1930's, the New Village plant was sending out one hundred railroad cars of cement a day. Edison built the first section of concrete highway in the Delaware Valley; it ran between the villages of Washington and Phillipsburg in New Jersey. He also designed and built houses made of poured concrete, and many of them are still lived in today. The biggest name in the industry, however, was not Edison; it was Alpha—or, more precisely, the Alpha Portland Cement Company.

Alpha operated large cement mills and limestone quarries at Martins Creek, Pennsylvania, on the banks of the Delaware. The Lehigh Portland Cement Company also had a plant nearby, and by 1910 these two companies employed all the available workers in this largely rural area. Alpha even built two company towns to attract arriving immigrants. One town was in Martins Creek, occupied mostly by Italian newcomers. The other was built in Brainards, New Jersey, just across the river from the plant. The place was originally named for David Brainerds (yes, it's spelled differently), a missionary to the Lenni-Lenape in the area during the mid-1790s. When the cement company took over, the place became a Slavic enclave in western New Jersey, its inhabitants walking to the plant in Pennsylvania over a railroad bridge. The hardy new Americans gave blood, sweat, and, sometimes, life itself to the Alpha. But those who are around today remember it as a good job and a good company.

Broad Street, the main thoroughfare in town, ran nearly to the river. Company houses lined this street, each with a small yard, at a rental of nine dollars a month. A water tower supplied running water to the village and some houses even had bathrooms inside. Broad Street also had a company store, a hotel (until it burned down in 1925), and always a tavern or two. Side streets held more company houses. There were a few boarding houses for single men, often run by widows whose husbands had been killed at the mills. Other women worked at the silk mills at Martins Creek.

The railroad ran on the river side of town and was part of the Pennsylvania Railroad's Bel-Del line, so called because it followed the Delaware River as far as Belvidere. In 1911 a tragic accident occurred here when an excursion train filled with schoolteachers on their way to Washington, DC, jumped a track under repair, rolled into a gully, and burst into flames. The wooden cars burned to ashes and thirteen people died, with another sixty seriously burned. In the 1920s the Pennsylvania Railroad took over the line and built a marshaling yard in town for cement and coal cars. People living close to the tracks remember the railyard as noisy and dirty. But this was

*Combination railroad and footbridge across the Delaware from Brainards, New Jersey,
to the Alpha Portland Cement Company in Martins Creek, Pennsylvania.
(Photo by Diana Dale)*

mitigated by the fact that the railroad built a station in the village
(which they oddly called "Martins Creek, New Jersey"), that was convenient for shopping trips to Phillipsburg.

Brainards also had a two-room schoolhouse on the outskirts of
town but no church. On Sundays people attended the Hungarian
church in Alpha, New Jersey, or the Greek Orthodox church, in
Phillipsburg.

The mills remained open during the Depression, except during a
seven-month strike in 1938 when the workers were fighting to
unionize. During World War II, they offered plenty of overtime.
Generally, life was pretty good in Brainards; everybody worked and
had a decent place to live, and there were always dances on weekends
at one of the local taverns. Most of the people were related by blood
or marriage, so the town was really like a big family.

Company houses, Brainards, New Jersey. (Photos by Frank Dale)

A gruesome break in this rather ordinary existence occurred on July 16, 1945. Ernest Rittenhouse, a local boy who married and moved to Orange, New Jersey, murdered his wife with an ax and disappeared. Police thought he might attempt to return to his boyhood home and the troopers set up a dragnet. Rittenhouse was finally captured across the bridge in Martins Creek. While being escorted back over the bridge in handcuffs by two troopers, he begged his captors to remove the uncomfortable cuffs. They complied and as the trio proceeded, Rittenhouse grabbed one of the trooper's guns and shot both men. One died, the other barely survived. The killer leaped off the bridge into the water and escaped. He was later recaptured, found to be insane, and put away for life.

By the 1960s both companies decided they could operate more efficiently and cheaply elsewhere. In 1960 Lehigh closed, and in 1964 Alpha followed. People found work at Ingersoll-Rand, a manufacturer of air compressors and air tools, or at various other plants in Easton and Phillipsburg. Alpha Cement, when it moved, sold the houses in Brainards to the tenants; nine hundred dollars for a house without indoor plumbing, twelve hundred dollars for one with a bathroom. Most folks bought their homes and stayed put.

Today, the unpretentious houses are neat and painted, their lawns like putting greens. One resident, John Dornich, took over the family tavern after his brother was killed in World War II. He tended bar part time while working at the mill, and he managed to put two sons through graduate school. He and his wife still live in the same house next to the now abandoned rail yards; she weeds among her flowers, he trims the grass along the railroad right-of-way and picks up litter that strangers throw there.

When they get together with neighbors, they talk of relatives who died or were maimed in coal dust explosions, quarry cave-ins, or train wrecks. Some among them recall the day in 1942 when twenty tons of dynamite went up at Lehigh Cement and atomized thirty-two workers, many from Brainards. And when they talk of World War II, one gets the impression that these Americans sacrificed inordinate numbers of their sons or husbands. Jim Dorcsis, now in his seventies,

After the Alpha Portland Cement Company shut down, John Dornich worked as a guard at the railroad crossing at Brainards. (Photo from the author's collection)

still carries German shrapnel in his body, but he says if he hadn't been in the army, he would have been at his job at Lehigh Cement in 1942 and would have died in the explosion with his friends.

Nobody boasts of the hardships they endured. These come out in the course of casual conversation, as if they were a normal part of life. There are no heroes here, just people who worked hard and played hard and went to church on Sunday.

15

THE
GREAT
CANOE
MARATHON

hat a year! In 1933 the world was in the throes of its worst-ever Depression; an Austrian paper-hanger had just become leader of Germany; Machine Gun Kelly was running amok out west; and a United States president known as FDR was teaching Americans a new alphabet—AAA, CCC, NRA, WPA—in an attempt to put millions of unemployed workers back on the job.

Harry E. Cudney of Hackettstown, New Jersey, was lucky. He had a job as protector for the New Jersey Fish and Game Commission. But even for him things were bad and getting worse. New Jersey's environment, like everything else in the world, was in serious decline. Worst of all, Cudney's beloved Delaware River was fast becoming a reeking sewer. Residents along its banks flushed their toilets into it; dye plants and paper mills colored its waters in rainbow hues. The river's eddies swirled with clots of wood pulp, foaming oily scum, and dead fish. Some longtime residents could remember shad runs in the river, and schoolchildren who listened to their tales of the mighty spring migrations with open-mouthed incredulity.

Harry Cudney knew that before anything could be done about cleaning up the river, the people of the state had to develop a concern that matched his own. What better way to get the ball rolling, he thought, than an event on the river that would draw thousands to its shores.

The idea he came up with in the summer of 1933 was a canoe race, a one-day dawn-to-dusk marathon. Tradition said that American Indians could cover sixty miles in this time span. Could modern day canoeists measure up? With the cooperation of his superiors at Fish and Game and their counterparts in Pennsylvania, the marathon received plenty of publicity. The American Canoe Association and canoe clubs from as far away as New York, Delaware, and Washington, DC, got involved. Local canoe buffs from both sides of the river became excited about the event.

Saturday, October 7, 1933, was selected as race day. The river should have sufficient water by then, and its wooded shores would be especially beautiful with autumn colors. The race would start at sunrise, officially 6:01 a.m., just upriver from the Phillipsburg-Easton Bridge at a place called Eddyside. It would end at sunset, 5:33 p.m., at which time rockets would be fired along the river. The remaining participants would then paddle to the nearest shore. There would be two categories of teams: all male and mixed male and female. The team from each category that traveled the greatest distance in the allotted time would win.

The rules were simple enough. Canoes had to be made of the usual canvas and wood, could measure no more than eighteen feet in length, and needed a team of two. One portage was mandatory: at Lambertville all canoes would go to the Pennsylvania shore and enter the canal there; the teams would then paddle down the canal until they had passed the wing dams and Wells Falls, then carry out to the river. Crews could make other portages as needed. Any team that got into trouble and required assistance would receive aid—then be disqualified. Each canoe could carry an extra paddle; there were no requirements concerning personal flotation devices.

Canoe clubs rushed to register, anxious to take part in what would be the last competition of the season. The Knickerbocker Canoe Club from New York entered its big guns: Mr. and Mrs. Leo Polt, and Bill Gaehlers and Mary Griffith. The Polts were fresh from a marathon victory in the Saint Lawrence River, and the Gaehlers-Griffith duo had been in the same event and had finished near the front. They were friendly but deadly serious competitors.

The Mohawk Canoe Club of Trenton sent John Mulcahy and Ray Pidcock. This pair, the oldest team in the race, had a combined age of 104, but nobody took them lightly.

Philadelphia's Cacawa Club entered three experienced teams. They were composed of Stanley Cimkowski and Frank Frick; Albert Bauer and Fletcher Holland; and Fred Wilke and John Haas Jr. These young Philadelphians were considered the ones to beat.

Easton's Riverside Canoe Club was well represented. Among its crews were forty-four-year-old Clyde Hester and his teammate, Billy "Wid" Jackson, a chain-smoking joker. Their canoe, really Hester's, was a seventeen-foot Old Town named *Rimdeer,* bought new in those deflated days for thirty-nine dollars. Other Riverside club members included Erwin "Stemmy" Stem and Norm Wolfinger, and Mr. and Mrs. Earle McMillan, Hester's neighbors in nearby Wilson.

A part-time Eastonite, Lafayette student Dick Stanhope, almost didn't make the race. His partner, a friend from Passaic, New Jersey, dropped out the day before the event. Then friends told Stanhope of a local canoeist, seventeen-year-old Rita Back, who, they thought, would love to be asked. Stanhope rushed to Easton High School, where Back was a senior; he got permission from the principal to get her out of class, and convinced the girl to be his partner. But first she had be excused from her Saturday job at the Easton five-and-dime. Unable to reach her employer, she arranged for one of her sisters to call the store the next morning and report Rita too sick to work.

Members of the Riverside Canoe Club, Easton, Pennsylvania, early 1930s. They are camped at Lake Hopatcong. William Jackson was in the great canoe marathon of 1933. He is the fifth person from the right holding the white flag. The fellow on the left in the white shirt is Clyde Hester, Jackson's partner in the marathon. (Photo courtesy of Virginia Jackson)

Dick and Rita had never been in a canoe together until the race began, but Rita, at least, had reason to be excited. She could now compete against her other sister, Frances, who had entered the race with Bob Svebda of Phillipsburg. Also, she had a favorable omen: she had been to a palm reader recently who said she would soon do something that would make her either famous or notorious.

Henry "Heinie" Kleedorfer, who lived at the edge of the river in Easton, joined forces with Frank "Baldy" Ball of Phillipsburg for the event, in spite of the fact that Eastonites considered "P'burgians" inferior canoeists. (The partnership would last, however; two years later the pair, with Heinie's kid brother, Bill, would launch a canoe in the Ohio River at Pittsburgh, Pennsylvania and paddle all the way to the Gulf of Mexico.)

As expected, many entrants were from New Jersey. Phillipsburg, in addition to "Baldy" Ball, was represented by Harold Tennicliff, John Slack, John Hough, Joe Glazier, George Snyder, Francis "Bat"

Rita Back at her high school graduation a few months after the 1933 marathon.
(Photo courtesy of Rita Back)

Masterson, Bob Myers, Matt Suttle, and others. Jack Painter, chief of police from the Flemington area, teamed up with Joe McQuillan, a professor at Haverford College. A tall, bespectacled boy from French-town, Howard Cooley, paired with his pal, Dick Bunch; they were the youngest team entered, with a combined age of thirty-five. (Cooley's grandfather had given them an old canoe for the race, which they spruced up with orange and black paint.) Homer Hicks was the best educated ice seller in Belvidere, having completed two years at Duke University before the hometown bank went under with what was left of his tuition money. Saturday was a busy day in the ice business, and he took it off reluctantly. He teamed with Al Lowe, a buddy from their days together in Boy Scouts.

Most of the New Jersey teams did not represent any canoe club. Instead, they were nonaffiliated amateurs, joined together only for this event and totally lacking in marathon experience and equipment. An unofficial competition developed between the canoe-club pros and these unsophisticated contestants in hand-me-down canoes. Some news reporters christened the New Jersey upstarts the "river rats." The name stuck.

Before dawn on Saturday, all of the ninety-four canoes formed an uneven line across the river, stretching from shore to shore. The pre-dawn weather was chilly, but the forecast called for a warm, sunny day. The last game of a hard-fought World Series between the New York Giants and the Washington Senators would take place later in the day, with the great Carl Hubbell on the mound. The weather gods had good reason to be kind.

Crowds stood two and three deep on the bridges at Phillipsburg, and more lined the riverbanks. Clyde Hester's family was on the first bridge; his son David remembers the starter's whistle and then the mad rush of canoes toward the shallow rapids at Getter's Island. He recalls that all the craft couldn't make it through the channel here at once, and that some got stuck or dumped, or were cut off and had to wait. When they all finally passed through this bottleneck, the flotilla spread out considerably. Below the crowded railroad bridge, a sharp bend in the river carried the paddlers from view and a second race began among the spectators, who ran for their cars to follow their favorites downriver.

For these fans, the next stop was Hoffman's Crossing at Carpentersville, where a high bank and a straight run of the river offered good viewing. Almost as quickly as the spectators shouldered into position here, the first canoe appeared through the early morning mist. It was boat number nine, paddled by Stanley Cimkowski and Frank Frick of Philadelphia's Cacawa Club. Each was kneeling on one knee in the prescribed marathon position. The canoe had covered the seven miles from the starting point in just fifty-two minutes.

Fred Wilke and John Haas, another Cacawa team, were in second place. Behind them, in third position, was a New York pair, Ernie Reidell and Les Krupa, but they were being pressed by the third Cacawa crew of Albert Bauer and Fletcher Holland. Back in the pack, a battle was shaping up between two mixed crews, the Polts and Gaehlers-Griffiths. They vied with each other for the lead in their category. Dick Stanhope and Rita Back, still getting used to each other, were well in the rear. Belvidere's Hicks and Lowe and Frenchtown's Cooley and Bunch remained in contention.

The first mishaps took place in the Carpentersville area. A large rock, barely submerged, snared a canoe, crew unidentified, and held it fast. In attempting to free their craft, the paddlers tore a sizeable hole in its canvas bottom and could not continue. Near the Riegelsville Bridge, a police patrol boat operated by Chick Melberger burst into flame for unknown reasons and had to be beached.

The next bridge, the one at Milford, was under repair, and workers blew a steam whistle to announce the appearance of the racers. Carloads of spectators, attempting to follow their heroes, were stymied by the closed span. Local police and state troopers on duty for river rescue had to instead unsnarl the ensuing traffic jam.

Spectators also packed the bridge at Frenchtown. A troop of Boy Scouts here attempted to record the positions of the canoes, and a bevy of local belles tossed confetti on the young favorites, Cooley and Bunch. Somebody more practical tossed the team lunch—the teenagers had forgotten to bring any.

Crowd on the Delaware River bridge at Riegelsville, Pennsylvania, watching canoes in the 1933 marathon. (Photo courtesy of Temple University Libraries, Urban Archives)

The front runners at Frenchtown as recorded by the Scouts were the three Philadelphia teams. The Cacawa Club had a lock on the lead and it was only eight o'clock in the morning. In the first two hours of the contest they had covered almost twenty miles.

Though these hard-driving young pros were forging ahead, those in the rear were still in the race. The battle between the Polts and Gaehlers-Griffiths remained intense, first one canoe taking the lead, then the other. They were too busy to notice Dick Stanhope and Rita Back closing in behind them. For a while, the Hicks and Lowe duo paddled side by side with the gray-haired Mulcahy and Pidcock. The two teams chatted awhile, then Mulcahy and Pidcock pulled ahead. And Chief Painter and the professor still ran strong.

By now the river's mist had dissipated, revealing the green and gold hills on either shore. As the sun climbed higher, the temperature

Fred Wilke and John Haas Jr., a Philadelphia team, pass through the inlet lock at New Hope, Pennsylvania. (Photo courtesy of Temple University Libraries, Urban Archives)

rose. It became a typical Indian summer day. Twenty-one-year-old "Stemmy" Stem of Easton's Riverside Club felt the heat of the sun on his head and wished he'd worn a hat. Before the race was over his scalp would be badly burned, and within months he would be bald, his only memento of the race. At Bull's Island, a canoe went over the wing dam and capsized. At the Lambertville portage, teams waited their turn to carry out of the canal and back into the river. A Jersey crew carried its craft around this waiting group gaining several places the easy way.

Below Lambertville, Homer Hicks and Al Lowe finally caught up with Mulcahy and Pidcock. The seniors were having lunch ashore, a fire heating water for tea. They waved.

At Scudders Falls, above Trenton, most crews located the chute between the wing dams and passed through unscathed, but one team missed the opening and took flight over the concrete obstruction.

The canoe broke in half on impact. The crew crawled ashore, embarrassed but unharmed.

Marathon officials had estimated that no one would get below Trenton in the allotted time. The city lay about sixty miles from the starting point, an outstanding day's canoeing. But at one o'clock that afternoon, marathon judges relaxing on the Delaware Bridge at Trenton were astounded to see a lone canoe threading its way among the river's boulders. Cimkowski and Frick, their kneeling position unchanged, paddled with strong and regular strokes—and they still had four more hours to go. Powerboats from the Trenton Yacht Club were commandeered, and excited officials, realizing they had made a colossal misjudgment, hurried downriver. Soon two more canoes appeared; Holland and Bauer had moved into second place, with Wilke and Haas in third position. It was the Philadelphians' day, indeed. Behind them, however, were many battlers who still considered it a race. Unfortunately, as the exhausted marathoners passed through the Trenton rapids, they entered tidewater—and the tide was moving upriver.

The Philadelphia teams detected it first, of course, and their aching bodies rebelled. The three canoes closed up and slowed perceptively. For some of the groups following, the tidewater proved the final blow. Already crippled with fatigue, they headed for the shore rather than struggle against this unexpected obstacle. About thirty-six of the starting crew persevered, however.

For the Polt and the Gaehlers-Griffiths teams, already worn out from their personal duel, the tidewater was more than they could handle. The Gaehlers-Griffiths craft went dead in the water, and Mary Griffiths collapsed in the bottom of the canoe. The Polts struggled ahead feebly. Stanhope and Back pressed on, fresher for having maintained a more measured pace, and they soon passed the stalled canoe. As she and Stanhope closed on the Polts, Rita Back thought she heard Mary Griffiths shouting encouragement to her. They soon passed the fading New Yorkers.

When the sunset rockets fired, the remaining teams paddled to the nearest shore. Stanley Cimkowski and Frank Frick made it to the

*Frank Frick (on left) and Stanley Cimkowski of Philadelphia, winners of the October
1933 canoe marathon in the Delaware River. This picture was taken in July 1939, when
they won a tandem senior race at the National Championships, Fountain Lake, New York
World's Fair. (Photo courtesy of Temple University Libraries, Urban Archives)*

Philadelphia city limits, eighty-six miles from the starting point.
They both had to be lifted from their canoe. The Bauer-Holland and
Wilke-Haas teams finished second and third, respectively. Dick Stanhope and Rita Back took first place in the mixed category, with Rita's
sister Frances and Frances's partner not far behind.

*Lafayette's Dick Stanhope holding victory trophy won by him and Rita Back in the 1933
canoe marathon. (Photo from the author's collection)*

Hicks and Lowe finished behind Mulcahy and Pidcock, but just
barely. Sunburned "Stemmy" Stem and Norm Wolfinger made it to the
end, as did many of the Phillipsburg contestants. Jackson and Hester
finished in eighteenth place; the chain-smoking Jackson hadn't taken
a puff the entire trip. The youngest team, Cooley and Bunch, finished
in a respectable twenty-sixth place. Chief Painter and Professor
McQuillan finished thirty-fourth, getting all the way to the Bristol
Bridge, a distance of seventy-five miles. The "river rats" had given a
good account of themselves.

At the ceremony at the Trenton Yacht Club that evening, all fin-
ishers ate a fine meal and each received a medal from the American
Canoe Association. George C. Warren Jr. of the New Jersey Fish and
Game Commission presented silver cups to the Cimkowski-Frick

team and to a beaming Dick Stanhope and Rita Back. Back also won a pair of silk stockings and an original oil painting. After the affair the contestants were transported back to Easton, their canoes deposited at Eddyside by the New Jersey Fish and Game Commission.

Monday's *Easton Express* proclaimed the Stanhope-Back victory in banner headlines, destroying Back's excuse with her boss for not coming to work on race day. When she went into work the next Saturday she found a pink slip waiting. Her palmist, thus, had been right on both counts.

For everyone else it had been a good day. Even for the hapless New Yorkers, Gaehlers-Griffiths and the Polts, the day wasn't a total washout. Their Giants won the World Series with a tenth inning homerun by Mel Ott.

But the biggest winner of all was Harry Cudney and his beloved river.

It had been the intention of the race organizers to make this event an annual affair, especially so after the success of the first one. For some reason this was not done. Certainly, the advent of World War II could be a partial explanation.

However, a race was finally scheduled for Columbus Day, October 12, 1946, some thirteen years after the initial contest. The rules were a little different: the canoes would start at Eddyside but would all finish up at the Trenton Yacht Club, handily avoiding another confrontation with the incoming tide. In addition to canoes, kayaks were welcome and would have their own category. And it would be a true race, rather than a marathon; there was a finish line and whoever crossed it first would be the winner. The distance covered would be 55 1/2 miles. Twenty-eight craft were entered, and the contestants included many mixed male and female teams (though this time they were not put into a separate category). Rain fell all day, and a strong upriver wind blew throughout the contest. The large and enthusiastic crowds of the first race were absent, but there were some similarities to the premier event. The Cacawa Club again entered the team of Frank Frick and John Haas. Names such as Masterson, Riedel, and

Kleedorfer were familiar from the first competition. Cacawa again won, with Frick and Haas finishing an hour ahead of the next team. Heinie Kleedorfer, teamed with his kid brother, Bill, won the second-place medal and brought glory to the upriver entrants.

This time the Easton paper gave little notice to the event, which was never held again.

16

THE BIG ONE OF '55

amn, *damn,* floozy!" one older resident called it. Maybe, in more innocent times, this seemed an adequate epithet for Hurricane Diane. Looking back to those August days of 1955, however, and the death and destruction the hurricane caused, one finds the designation much too mild. Besides, Diane wasn't the only one.

Hurricane Connie, after much indecision, came ashore in North Carolina on August 12, 1955. Winds of one hundred miles per hour and torrential rains hit this southern area, but the weather bureau did not think it would continue to the northeast and cancelled the hurricane warnings for that region. Parenthetically, it noted a new storm forming five hundred miles north-northeast of San Juan, Puerto Rico, which it named Diane.

Connie was deceptive, however. It turned north, smashed into the mid-Atlantic states, moved east to west across New Jersey into Pennsylvania, and finally expired over Lake Erie, leaving forty people dead. Ten inches of rain fell in the Delaware Valley in two days, soaking the ground and putting the rivers near flood stage. But the month before, July, had been the driest in this area in fifty years, so many residents welcomed the water. Unfortunately, the second half of a one-two punch was about to land.

In the early morning of August 17, Diane hit the Carolinas in the area already hammered by Connie a few days before. Hurricane warnings extended north to Delaware Bay. Beyond that, only heavy rain was predicted.

Thursday, August 18, dawned dark and ominous in the Delaware Valley. There was almost no wind. The rain, heading north, had increased in intensity during the night. In Sussex and Warren counties in northwestern New Jersey, six inches of rain fell overnight. Across the river in eastern Pennsylvania, in the Pocono Mountains resort area, ten inches of rain fell that day and into the night. With the ground already saturated and the streams flooded, the effect proved disastrous.

Camp Davis was located on the shores of Brodhead Creek at Analomink, near Stroudsburg, Pennsylvania. A pleasant trout stream that eventually finds its way to the Delaware, the Brodhead is fed by the Pocono watershed. The camp was run by a retired Baptist minister, the Reverend Leon Davis, and it catered to religious families. Most of the guests came from northern New Jersey—mothers and their children, with the fathers coming to visit mostly on the weekends.

As the waters rose, the campers left their cabins and gathered in the main building, a two-story frame structure. Another camp, Pine Brook, lay on higher ground a mere one hundred yards distant, but the Camp Davis people underestimated their danger and stayed put. The turbulent waters continued to mount and the terrified campers were forced up to the second floor and then finally to the attic, where they huddled in the dark and prayed. Friends from Pine Brook could hear their screams and calls for help but were powerless. Then the building disintegrated in a thirty-foot wall of water and all forty-six campers, most of them children, were swept away. Nine were later found alive, clinging to tree limbs or debris, or having been miraculously swept ashore. Some bodies were never recovered.

The bridge that linked the boroughs of Stroudsburg and East Stroudsburg lies wrecked along the banks of Brodhead Creek. Waters from this swollen creek smashed into Camp Davis downstream and killed thirty-seven. Only nine campers survived. (Photo courtesy of the Express-Times, *Easton, Pennsylvania)*

One survivor, Irene Weber of West Paterson, New Jersey, left the camp for an hour or two to visit friends. She returned to discover she had lost her son, her daughter, her mother, her sister, her brother-in-law, a niece, and a nephew.

Jennie Johnson of Jersey City was at the camp with her two sons, Roy and David, and a daughter, Nancy. They too sought refuge in the main house and retreated to the attic as the water rose. She recalled:

> The house gave a shudder and collapsed and forty of us went tumbling in a jumble of water, boards, and screams. It was dark and I could hear the children calling but I couldn't help them. I went under and something must have hit my head. . . . I passed out. I came to and grabbed a board and then I was tossed on an island of debris, branches and boards, floating on the water. I heard a voice very close. It was Beth Liddle, I knew her family from camp. . . . I reached out and touched her and we held on to each other and cried every time we heard a child in the distance calling for help."

The two were eventually saved by a man in a motorboat. Johnson lost both her sons, but her daughter survived. Eleven-year-old Beth lost her mother, her brother, and other relatives.

Other sites also suffered, though without as many casualties. Camp Miller was a Lutheran camp on the banks of the Delaware, just north of Shawnee. The camp was demolished, but about 260 boys, led by slightly older counselors, waded through the waist-deep flood. Linked together arm-in-arm, they all reached higher ground safely. Several other camps were also evacuated without incident. The State of Pennsylvania, in an operation dubbed Kid-Lift, transported ten thousand children from endangered summer camps in eastern Pennsylvania to their homes.

Before it enters the Delaware, Brodhead Creek passes through both Stroudsburg and East Stroudsburg. The smaller East Stroudsburg was completely cut off for many days, and several of its citizens who lived in a creekside area called "Silk Mill Flats" were carried away with their homes and drowned. Elsewhere in the town, Thursday night bingo was in full swing at the Day Street fire hall. So intent were the players that they didn't notice the rising flood until too late. The wall of water, which demolished Camp Davis upstream, now smashed into the frame building and killed six.

The Delaware, Lackawanna & Western Railroad, principal freight and passenger carrier across eastern Pennsylvania and northern New Jersey, took devastating losses, especially from the Poconos to the Delaware Water Gap. T. T. Taber, unofficial historian for the railroad, wrote, "Locked between washouts were two passenger trains carrying three hundred people, and four freight trains carrying perishables and other freight needed by consignees. Sixty miles of track—main line and yard—were wrecked. Several large bridges and culverts went down the stream. Embankments and roadbeds disappeared completely for several miles." The following year the DL&W petitioned the courts for reorganization and soon went out of business, unable to recover from the catastrophe.

While Pennsylvanians were tragically counting bodies, New Jerseyites were experiencing miracles. The Belvidere Ambulance and Rescue Squad was out on the river before sunrise on Thursday morning, responding to the cries of terrified vacationers living in cottages on Thomas and Manunka Chunk islands. Their own boats had been swept away by rising waters. The squad's boat, crewed by Lew Jones and Nels Darymple, made repeated trips in the debris-filled river to rescue some fifty of the trapped summer residents.

At Camp St. Vincent in Pahaquarry Township, John Uporsky and neighbor Rudy Schenk operated their outboard boats to evacuate seventy orphaned boys on vacation from a Brooklyn institution. They and their priest—counselors were trapped on the roofs of cabins. On the way in, Uporsky had plucked from a tree two boys who had attempted, unsuccessfully, to flee the rising water in a truck. Soon the truck was under water eight feet deep and rising. Uporsky remembered, "The water was so high I was ducking under wires and cross-

In this East Stroudsburg building, one hundred women were playing bingo when a wall of water smashed into it, killing several of the players. (Photo courtesy of the Express-Times, *Easton, Pennsylvania)*

members of power poles." Later, Belvidere's rescue boat arrived at the camp, fresh from its efforts downriver, with a crew consisting of Jones, Darymple, Cliff Griffin, and a state trooper named Gaylord. They took two flood victims, priests, off the roof. As they got going the boat's overworked engine quit, and the craft was swamped. The desperate men swam to a nearby baseball backstop and clung to it. Griffin struggled to keep one priest afloat until an army-surplus amphibious "duck" arrived and took them aboard. Days later, members of the squad recovered their craft.

At Flatbrookville, a settlement in Sussex County nearly surrounded by the Delaware and the Flat Brook, the Behrenburg family—father, mother, and three children—awoke in their isolated vacation cabin to find the floor covered with several inches of muddy water. Because the cabin was on a knoll, the distraught father feared attempting an escape on foot. Then he looked out a window on the upstream side of the house and saw an errant canoe bobbing in the flood. He secured the craft and loaded his family into it, fully intent on escaping even without benefit of a paddle. Then . . . a paddle came floating by. The father got his family to high ground and safety. The cabin washed away.

At Branchville, also in Sussex County, a babbling stream wound through this village of eight hundred residents. Known as Culvers Brook, it had two dams on it: a mill dam and, just upstream, a larger dam that at one time had been used to generate electricity for the town. The large lake behind the dam was appropriately named Electric Pond. The Electric Pond dam collapsed at about 5 A.M. on the nineteenth, causing the second, smaller dam to be swept away and a ten-foot wave of water, laced with trees and cars, to smash through the center of the village like a bulldozer gone mad, taking out houses, bridges, and stores. It even undermined about a mile of the DL&W Railroad track and a modern four-lane state highway bridge. Fortunately, an alert fire company sounded a fire whistle and saved many lives.

Dean McNeillie evacuated his family from their home on the stream's bank, but he and his brother-in-law, J. D. Reed, stayed behind to pump out the cellar. They hastily deserted this job when they heard the fire whistle's warning and raced up a gently sloping hill toward higher ground. The water caught them but, young and strong, they managed to swim and avoid dangerous floating debris. Finally, they regained their footing and waded ashore. A minister was on his way to tell Mrs. McNeillie that she had lost a husband and a brother when he came upon the benumbed pair.

Although water reached its second floor, the family's one hundred-year-old house survived, though a porch, some outbuildings, and a grove of old oaks and maples that had surrounded it did not. Forty years later, Mrs. McNeillie still had trouble with silt filtering out of electric wall sockets.

A couple of local men were out on the streets of Branchville at this early hour. O. J. Fields owned a grocery store in town and was driving around checking on conditions. The wave caught him in his car and pushed the vehicle backwards down Mill Street. He got out, climbed a tree, and clung there above the swirling water.

Charles Culver was walking on Mill Street when he saw the wave coming toward him. He hid behind a huge tree, hugging it, and watched mangled cars rolling end over end on either side of his refuge.

Elsewhere in Sussex County, roads and bridges leading into Sussex Borough were washed out, leaving the village totally isolated until the U.S. Army Corps of Engineers installed a temporary bridge a week later. Clove Brook, which flows into the borough from the mountains of High Point, followed its serpentine course under Route 23, washing out every bridge along the way.

By late Friday morning, the rain had stopped, the sun shone, and temperatures were climbing to record levels. In the Delaware Valley below Stroudsburg, nobody realized what had happened upriver or that the river's waters would crest at catastrophically higher levels before the day was over.

At Portland, Pennsylvania, the river had risen by morning to the decking of the century-old covered bridge, the only wooden bridge that had survived the terrible Pumpkin Freshet of October 1903. The bridge tender, Charles Newbaker, had been on the job here for fifty years and lived with his family in a riverside house perched high on a stone levee nearby. When the family awoke, the river was lapping at the back door.

Newbaker's daughter, Hilda, recalled, "Trucks came to evacuate us. We almost took too long gathering possessions. When we finally left, the water was coming in through the windows. We had to wade to the trucks . . . but the bridge was still there when we left."

The seventy-five-year-old bridge tender remained on duty after his family departed and was there, in uniform, to watch the destruction of the historic span.

Neil Brodt, a young barber living in Portland, witnessed the main street beginning to flood that morning. As a volunteer firefighter, he helped evacuate people living in the little riverside business district and carried the cash drawers from the post office in thigh-deep water. He then borrowed a pickup truck and took coffee upriver to Civil Defense workers, who were involved in the search for survivors of Camp Davis. When he returned a short time later the covered bridge was gone—an eyewitness told him a bungalow floating down the river had hit the center span—and water had reached the second floor of most Main Street buildings. The Portland National Bank stood in fifteen feet of water, its vault and safe deposit boxes submerged.

The summer resort at Hutchinson, below Belvidere, washed away in the flood. Most of the cottages and year-round homes at Foul Rift, Harmony Station, Manunka Chunk, Martins Creek, and Sandts Eddy were lost or badly damaged.

Paul and Betty Conrad lived at Depue's Ferry, Pennsylvania, just downriver from the power plant at Martins Creek. Betty Conrad worked for the telephone company in Belvidere and received a frantic call at home on the nineteenth to come in to work, but already the roads were awash and she couldn't get out. Instead, she got on a party line and called neighbors to warn them to evacuate. The Conrads saw the lights of police cars across the river at Hutchinson as residents were being rescued from that ill-fated community. As their houses began to fill with water, the Conrads moved all their furniture to the second floor and then beat a hasty retreat. The next morning they returned by motorboat and found the river had risen to the second floor. They climbed in through a window and moved all the furniture to the attic, where it remained safe and dry.

The Conrads later remembered the help local farmers provided to people. The high-clearance farm tractors got around well in the floodwater and, with a wagon attached, were ideal for transporting goods or people to high ground. The Conrads also never forgot the mud in their home, even on the ceiling and in the light fixtures. The smell, emanating from a composite of septic tank overflow, dead animals, rotted food, and fertilizer, returned for years afterward, especially on damp days.

The historic covered bridge at Columbia, New Jersey, is swept away in the Hurricane Diane flood of 1955. (Photo courtesy of Neil Brodt)

Dick Harpster, a *Newark Evening News* reporter, went on a rescue mission with the state police on the morning of the nineteenth. The group, in a police launch, headed for the islands near Manunka Chunk, unaware that they had already been evacuated by the Portland and Belvidere squads. Harpster would later remember his calmness as the boat passed over the flooded cornfields, and his shock when it reached the river. The roiling waters bristled with trees, houses, boats, and dead animals; soon, huge sections of the Columbia covered bridge floated by. Harpster became convinced that when this debris-laden crest hit the two Phillipsburg bridges they would sunder like kindling. Anticipating some spectacular pictures, he arranged for a photographer to stand by at Phillipsburg. The higher toll bridge there remained above the flood's crest—although its approaches became impassable—but the lower, older free bridge connecting Phillipsburg and Easton was gutted, its steel beams twisted like spaghetti. Unfortunately for posterity, it happened after dark and the photographer missed his shots.

Verne Steinmann, a New Jersey state trooper, was stationed at the Clinton barracks. He drove to work on the sunny morning of the nineteenth with no indication of any unusual problems. When he arrived at Clinton, he and a partner were rushed to the Blairstown area, where it was feared camps here might have suffered the same fate as those in the Poconos. The troopers found Route 46 flooded at Manunka Chunk. Steinman and his partner followed backroads to Hainesburg, crossing the raging Paulinskill River on a bridge that was awash. Then, instructed over the car radio to return to Clinton, the troopers recrossed the bridge. Looking back after this crossing, the men saw the bridge shift off its footings. Theirs would be the last crossing here for a while.

The Jungle Zoo, located on Route 46 in Manunka Chunk, also was awash. It was owned by Ivan Sanderson, who had achieved considerable fame appearing on TV with his animals—especially "Jocko the Croc," a seven-foot Cuban crocodile. When the zoo became flooded, most of the inmates were freed and taken elsewhere by two employees, Edgar Schoenberger and Patricia Vanatta. But the pair

were a little concerned about how to handle Jocko. Finally, Shoen-
berger swam to Jocko's cage and, with a pair of wire cutters, cut a
hole in the fencing and let the croc escape. After several weeks of
fruitless searching, Jocko was given up for lost. Then, in October,
Betty Conrad at DePue's Ferry found strange impressions and tracks
in the sand at the river's edge. Then she saw Jocko, who had been lured
across the river by the warm water discharged by the power plant.
Schoenberger arrived with a lasso and retrieved the celebrity croc.

The people of Phillipsburg and Easton went to work that morning of the nineteenth, pleased to see a clear day. Those who crossed
either of the two bridges were amazed at the height of the water but
assumed the worst was over. At this time, however, the river was only
nine feet above flood stage. Before the day was over, the Delaware at
Phillipsburg would rise an astounding forty-three feet, a full ten feet
above the level set in the fabled flood of 1903.

Charles Brogan of Phillipsburg, home on leave from the army,
was marrying an Easton girl the next day. He drove across the free
bridge at 9 A.M., picked up tuxedos for the wedding party, and did
some additional shopping. When he attempted to return via the same
bridge, he found it underwater. Finally, he abandoned his car and
waded through armpit-deep water to get to the still-intact toll bridge
and return home. His next crossing would be on the much higher
railroad bridge, a route used by many people in the next few days.
Some of the wedding party never arrived, and the Easton hotel,
where the reception was to be held, had been flooded up to the second floor. But love, as it usually does, conquered all. (At last report
the marriage has prospered, and the couple have had eight little Bro-
gans along the way.)

Ronald Wynkoop of Phillipsburg went to work that morning at
his job at Baker Chemical. Soon, rising water made work impossible
and he climbed to the roof, where he spent time watching the river.
Then, realizing his danger, he beat a hasty retreat. Later, when the
flood was over, he was approached by a young Marine from Little
Falls, New Jersey, who wanted help finding a sister who had been at
Camp Davis. Wynkoop went to the Stroudsburg area several times to

The free bridge between Easton and Phillpsburg, looking toward Northampton Street, Easton. The river is at its crest. (Photo courtesy of Carl R. Baxter)

aid the young man. They searched through brush-filled ravines, collapsed buildings, and all the morgues that had been set up in the area—to no avail.

Debris watching became a favorite occupation for those who had nothing better to do. Some older residents insisted they saw complete stills floating by. Verne Steinman witnessed a twenty-two-foot cabin cruiser, new-looking and without anyone on board, converted to kindling when it hit a bridge. Whole houses, large trees, trailers, and fuel tanks filled the river and made any kind of boat travel extremely hazardous. This flotsam battered the free bridge at Phillipsburg and finally destroyed it during the night of August 19–20. Another Delaware River bridge downstream at Byram–Point Pleasant met the same fate.

The free bridge over the river at Easton after the flood of August 1955.
(Photo courtesy of Carl R. Baxter)

Although boat travel on the river was very risky, those whose job it was to save lives took chances. Both Easton and Phillipsburg fire-fighters braved the flood in rowboats and pulled people from threatened homes. Harvey Wismer of Phillipsburg had a twenty-four-foot craft with an outboard motor, and Wayne Frick, from the Pennsylvania side of the river, owned a war-surplus amphibious vehicle. They, with some helpers, saved 110 people on the first day of the flood. Many similar feats went unheralded.

Downstream from Phillipsburg and Easton things were no better. Carpentersville was virtually wiped out, with 83 of its 89 residences lost. Phillipsburg National Guard members, Alpha firefighters, and a troop of Explorer Scouts rushed there. Civil Defense agencies, created to deal with a Soviet nuclear attack, were indispensible.

At Frenchtown, several houses and plants built along the river washed away, but most of the homes had been built on higher ground and survived. The Kerr Chicken Company there lost four hundred thousand chicks in incubators when the power went out. And though the deck of the bridge between Frenchtown and Pennsylvania lay underwater, the span held.

At Raubsville, Milford, Upper Black Eddy, Lambertville, and New Hope, the story was the same: homes gone, electricity gone, phones gone. There was plenty of water, all of it contaminated.

Most residents in Riegelsville, Pennsylvania, abandoned their homes. A shelter and kitchen were set up at St. Peter's Church, located there on a hill. The food was so good at the kitchen that New Jersey State troopers, on duty 'round the clock, crossed the river into Pennsylvania to eat there.

By the time the crest of the flood reached Trenton, it had lost some of its force. Nevertheless, state employees erected sandbag dikes in the rear of the Assembly Building. (Ironically, lawmakers inside were voting a drought-control measure to deal with the excessively dry conditions that had prevailed earlier in the summer.)

By Saturday, the twentieth, the water was receding. Some people were able to return to their homes, but over three thousand New Jersey residents and an equal number from across the river had no homes to return to. An oily film of silt covered everything up to a depth of one foot, and a terrible stench—an aroma of feces and rotten flesh—suffocated the region.

If there is any good memory of this tragedy, it is that of people helping people. In Branchville, after McNeillie had returned to his house, his boss arrived and, while water was still running out the windows, went to work with some friends mopping, shoveling, hammering, and sawing until the house was habitable—all while the exhausted McNeillie slept.

In Easton, Mennonites had arrived on the nineteenth, unasked, to help with the cleanup and with feeding the hungry, They stayed until both jobs were done.

In Belvidere, the mayor's wife and some neighbors set up a kitchen in the Masonic Hall. They ladled out stew and similar hearty

The August 1955 flood aftermath—houses along the riverbank in Carpentersville, New Jersey. (Photos courtesy of Carl R. Baxter)

fare to the hungry, and housed the homeless for weeks. While doing this, they also found time to send food to stricken Stroudsburg.

Such stories abounded. A man from Long Island rented a helicopter and flew to Pennsylvania to rescue children from a flood-threatened camp. Parents whose children were lost at Camp Davis helped other parents find theirs. Not a fire company, rescue squad, Red Cross unit, Scout troop, nor church group was found wanting.

President Dwight D. Eisenhower made a trip to the flood zone, and Congress eventually voted 100 million dollars in aid for the area (the final cost far exceeded this amount). The proposal to build a dam across the free-flowing Delaware to prevent a recurrence of such a flood received impetus by this calamity. The death toll as a result of the twin hurricanes climbed to four hundred, the most shocking of which were the young children swept to their doom in the dark of night on Brodhead Creek.

The last to die as a direct result of the flood was George Stanko. Several days after Hurricane Diane had passed, he attempted to cross the ruined free bridge at Phillipsburg by walking on a bundle of phone cables strung temporarily over the river. He fell into the swirling current and, before anyone could reach him, disappeared—a tragic denouement to the greatest natural disaster to hit the Delaware Valley in recorded history.

17

THE BATTLE FOR TOCKS ISLAND

he flood was the catalyst. After the two hurricanes, Connie and Diane, struck the Delaware Valley and water levels in the river set new records, the outcry for help and preventive measures were immediate and loud.

After several years of surveys by the U.S. Army Corps of Engineers, Congress passed the Flood Control Act of 1962. This law provided for a huge main-stem dam at Tocks Island, six miles upriver from the Delaware Water Gap. The dam would contain a lake thirty-seven miles long, extending all the way to Port Jervis, New York. A national park called the Delaware Water Gap National Recreation Area would also be established, increasing the total area of the project to seventy-two thousand acres, with most of the land to be purchased or taken by condemnation from local owners. The Army Corps of Engineers, the project's designers and builders, estimated that 10 1/2 million visitors a year would come to the 80-square-mile park, making it the busiest national park in the United States. (By comparison, Yellowstone with 3,472 square miles had an annual visitation of 2.4 million people.) So grandiose were some of the corps'

Artist's conception of proposed Tocks Island Dam. (Courtesy of Nancy Shukaitis, President, Delaware Valley Conservation Association)

schemes that a few of the early dam advocates began to have second thoughts. Their numbers would soon multiply.

Hydroelectric power from the dam's waters would be produced by a consortium of private power companies, which would have water storage facilities and turbines located on the top of nearby Kittatinny Mountain. The power companies—Jersey Central Power and Light, Public Service Electric, and New Jersey Power and Light—had purchased parkland atop the mountain from the State of New Jersey in 1961, with the approval of Governor Robert Meyner. This property included one of New Jersey's few glacial lakes, Sunfish Pond. The consortium planned to increase the size of the pond and use it as its upper storage reservoir. A lower reservoir would be built at Yards Creek on the other side of the mountain, with turbines between the two.

Hackettstown's Casey Kays first saw Sunfish Pond in August 1961. His immediate reaction was a prayer: "Oh God, thank you for this." The Appalachian Trail skirts its shores, and the pond had become a legendary part of that two thousand-mile path. When the sale of the pond became generally known in 1965, Kays and fellow naturalist Glenn Fisher were furious that this treasure, part of the public domain, had been sold off by the politicians without any open discussion. Operating independently of each other at first, they both began writing letters and getting signatures on petitions to forestall the destruction of the pond. Fisher and a few friends formed the Lenni-Lenape League, which Kays soon joined.

Fisher's well-reasoned letters appeared regularly in the *New York Times* and other national publications. These and a deluge of petitions began to have an effect. A few members of Congress spoke out against the use of the pond and a little-known New Jersey assemblyman and future governor, Tom Kean, gave his active support to the Lenni-Lenape League. On May 18, 1966, a well-publicized hike to the pond, a twelve-mile round trip, produced 655 signatures on a petition in spite of heavy rains. In June of the next year more than a thousand hikers and reporters, led by sixty-eight-year-old Supreme Court Justice William O. Douglas, made another pilgrimage to the pond. Douglas's words, "Sunfish Pond is a unique spot and deserves to be preserved," made headlines in the national press the next day. Douglas followed up with a scalding article in *Playboy* attacking the whole Tocks Island project, the opening sentence of which read: "The Army Corps of Engineers is public enemy number one."

F. J. Trembley, an ecology professor at Lehigh University, feared that the siphoning of water for the hydropower operations would cause wide fluctuations in water levels in the thirty-seven-mile reservoir and pose a danger to fish and their spawn. His dire predictions brought those who enjoyed sportfishing into the fray. And when the National Park Service, and integral part of the Tocks Island project, came out publicly against the destruction of Sunfish Pond, pressure mounted on the consortium to abandon that portion of its plans. On July 1, 1969, Sunfish Pond was sold back to the state, and a year later it was placed in the Registry of National Landmarks. Casey Kays, Glenn Fisher, and their little army had won the first battle.

But they weren't done yet. Since they had learned of the project, these activists—part of a new but growing movement called environmentalism—had been fighting the entire Tocks Island dam and reservoir concept. The international situation in the mid-sixties seemed to bolster their position. The United States was in an escalating war in Vietnam, and President Lyndon Johnson had called on Congress to control non-military expenditures so that more could be spent on the war effort. Hence, the Army Corps of Engineers' budget for Tocks Island (which would rise from $90 million in 1962 to a whopping $400 million in 1975, exclusive of the recreation project) came under close scrutiny. The national park feature, with its promise of 10 1/2 million paying visitors a year, had been intended to make the Tocks Island project more cost effective. But many critics felt that the corps had exaggerated these figures in an attempt to regain waning Congressional support.

For the same reason, critics said, the corps had kept its land acquisition costs to a minimum. Corps appraisers, negotiating with landowners, had offered extremely low prices for homesteads and farms. Also, they had been accused of using intimidation to force these rural people into accepting; to the corps, driving a hard bargain was more important than fairness. And some of the landowners couldn't grasp the logic of permanently flooding twelve thousand acres behind the dam to prevent the occasional deluge downstream of a ten thousand-acre floodplain. Some openly resented having to give up their farms and homes to provide city people with a place to play.

In 1967 Dick Harpster, a Warren County resident and reporter for the *Newark Evening News,* received a call from a group of homeowners who were scheduled to be moved by the Army Corps of Engineers. He attended their meeting and was appalled at what he heard. Mina Haefele of Pahaquarry told of being offered a below-market price for her place and, when she didn't bite, being threatened with the destruction of the road on which she lived—no school bus or ambulance would be able to reach her house. Still she refused to settle. Another owner was told by the corps that he could expect fire insurance to be cancelled on his place, since fire trucks couldn't get to his house on the unmaintained roads.

Appraisers discouraged any appeal of their offers; the appeal would take years, they said, and lawyers and private appraisers would

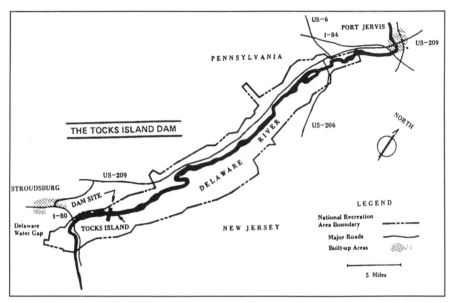

Location of the proposed Tocks Island Dam. (Map courtesy of the
Save the Delaware Coalition)

eat up any gain. The corps insisted some sellers leave at once, although it would be years before the area was flooded; the early
evictees included a blind man in his seventies. The corps' practice of
splitting a landholding proved a special hardship to the valley's farmers; the government would buy that portion of a farm in the recreation area but postpone buying the remaining portion in the reservoir
area. Thus, a farmer would be left with a house but no acreage to
work, or with acreage but no house in which to live. One despairing
landowner committed suicide. Others wept openly at public meet-
ings; some threatened to shoot any appraiser who came near. Eventually eight thousand residents were moved out. Dick Harpster became
their spokesperson, writing articles regularly about this situation. The
corps officials threatened him and even went to see his editor in
Newark, but Harpster eventually prevailed.

Across the river, Pennsylvania landowners had been subjected to
the same trials. Nancy Shukaitis's family had lived on a riverside farm
since the eighteenth century. After the big 1955 flood, her husband

The Army Corps of Engineers won few popularity contests at Tocks Island.
(Photo courtesy of Richard Harpster)

had carried bodies from nearby Brodhead Creek. Now they were going to lose their farm to the project. The first and only opponent at a
1964 congressional hearing, this embattled woman had spoken out.
In the beginning, she was a voice crying in the wilderness, but not
for long. At a House of Representatives hearing in Washington later
that year, some members of the House came to her support.

In 1965 Shukaitis had formed the Delaware Valley Conservation
Association (DVCA). This anti-Tocks organization grew to have more
than a thousand members, many of whom were the same people
Harpster had been championing. When Shukaitis was elected to the
Monroe County Commission, the county's governing body, others
took over the DVCA, including Mina Haefele and Sandy McDonald,
both Jerseyans. The DVCA newsletter, the *Minisink Bull,* along with
the Lenni-Lenape League's *Lenape Smoke Signals* and Harpster's flood
of newspaper articles, began to have an impact. National conservation groups such as the Sierra Club, the National Wildlife Federation,
the American Canoe Club, and Trout Unlimited, together with the

Nancy Shukaitis fought the Tocks Island Dam from the beginning, even appearing before Congress on many occasions. (Photo courtesy of Nancy Shukaitis, President, Delaware Valley Conservation Association)

Lenni-Lenape League and the Delaware Valley Conservation Association, united to form the Save the Delaware Coalition. Led by Harold A. Lockwood, a Philadelphia lawyer and activist, this umbrella organization became strong enough to command the respect of Congress. Indeed, when the coalition spoke, everybody listened.

During this period a growing awareness of environmental issues developed nationally. Army Corps of Engineers projects came under attack all over the United States. A proposed corps dam across the beautiful Red River Gorge in Kentucky was dropped in March 1969 after a long battle by conservationists, capped by a weekend anti-dam march at the gorge led by arch-foe Justice William O. Douglas. The Sewell Bluff Dam in Georgia was stopped in 1973 by Governor Jimmy Carter, who referred to "a growing awareness of the value of . . . irreplaceable natural resources." At a dam on the Missouri River near Niobrara, Nebraska, silt build-up behind the structure backed into the town like some science-fiction "Blob," forcing the town's permanent abandonment and further increasing environmental awareness.

In January 1970 the National Environmental Policy Act became the law of the land. It made all projects of the Army Corps of Engineers and others subject to substantial environmental controls. The Council of Environmental Quality (CEQ) administered the act and was particularly concerned with something called eutrophication, the pollution of water by runoff that contains manure and other fertilizers. This form of pollution causes the rapid growth of algae in unmoving waters such as lakes and reservoirs, and it soon depletes the water of oxygen. Later the New Jersey Medical Society warned that this same form of pollution would introduce high levels of deadly salmonella into the reservoir. The corps replied with an environmental impact statement of unusual frankness. It quoted its consulting engineer, Jack McCormick, in part: "Accelerated difficulties are likely to occur after creation of the proposed Tocks Island Lake."

The CEQ passed this on to the secretary of the army and added its own opinion that the drawdown of water from the reservoir to operate turbines, for example, would create acres of mud flats behind the dam, something anti-Tocks groups had been saying for years.

Meanwhile, in Warren County, New Jersey, and Monroe County, Pennsylvania, voter referenda indicated local citizens were dead set against the dam. Warren County freeholders Ray Stem of Phillipsburg and Ben Bosco of Belvidere were elected, in part, because of their opposition to the project. Then, a four-county task force on the Tocks Island Dam was established by Warren and Sussex county freeholders in New Jersey and Pike and Monroe county commissioners in Pennsylvania, with one delegate from each county. They met monthly in alternating courthouses to examine and publicly discuss issues relating to the project.

Finally, New Jersey's Governor William Cahill sent to Congress a whole list of conditions that would have to be met to keep his state's support. He especially asked for financial aid from the federal government to build roads and other services to accommodate the millions of visitors to the new national park, and he wanted the number of those visitors limited to 4 million rather than 10 1/2 million. Meanwhile, officials in the State of Delaware were becoming concerned that an increase in salinity, caused by a decrease in fresh water coming down the river, would destroy its oyster beds in Delaware Bay.

With all this encouragement, the Save the Delaware Coalition increased its lobbying. It also issued several reports that it submitted to Congress, one of which recommended the park idea be retained, albeit on a smaller scale, but the river remain free-flowing—no dam. In the summer of 1974 the National Park Service began drawing up tentative plans for such a park. And in August of the same year, New Jersey's new governor, Brendan T. Byrne, led a canoe caravan down the river to Tocks Island with a gaggle of reporters and TV crews paddling along behind. Representative Helen Meyner, wife of the governor who had sold off Sunfish Pond, was there pledging her support. On the island the governor expressed his love of the valley as it was and insisted on satisfactory answers to environmental questions, without which he would withhold his support of the project.

A turning point came when the governors of the four states in the valley and a representative of the Department of the Interior met in Newark, New Jersey, in July 1975. They voted 3-1 against further funding for the Tocks Dam, with the Department of the Interior abstaining. Only Pennsylvania held out for what was fast becoming a lost cause.

A short time later the Army Corps of Engineers, bowing to the inevitable, joined other groups in requesting that Congress deauthorize the dam. Congress, preferring not to set a legal precedent in deauthorizing a public works project, did nothing.

If any further ammunition against the dam were needed, the collapse in 1976 of the corps-built, earth-and-rockfill Teton Dam in Idaho provided it. This dam held much less water than the Tocks Island Dam would and it drained into a mostly rural area; nevertheless, several small towns were wiped out and eleven people lost their lives. The Save the Delaware Coalition quickly pointed out that the Tocks Dam would be built on unstable glacial material and a collapse would send a surge of water smashing through the many densely populated areas downstream.

New Jersey's governor, Brendan Byrne, and friends look over the dam site at Tocks Island.
(Photo courtesy of Richard Harpster)

Not content to wait for Congress to reach a decision on deauthorization, environmental groups tried to have the middle section of the river, where the reservoir and dam would be, included in the National Wild and Scenic Rivers System. In the spring of 1977, rookie representative Peter Kostmayer from Pennsylvania introduced such a bill in the House, and Senator Clifford Case from New Jersey did the same in the Senate. The bill Congress finally passed effectively blocked the building of the dam on this stretch of the river, and it was signed into law by a smiling President Jimmy Carter on November 10, 1978. The Tocks Island Dam was dead; a national recreation area around a free-flowing Delaware emerged the victor. Deauthorization was only a formality now, finally becoming official on July 19, 1992.

The story of the rise and fall of the Tocks Island project mirrors the times in which it occurred. The immediate and unanimous demand for a dam after the 1955 flood reflected a pre-war attitude toward rivers expressed by President Herbert Hoover in 1928: "Every drop [of river water] which runs to the sea without yielding its full economic service is a waste."

But beginning in the 1960s, attitudes toward water resources and the environment in general started to change. People began to realize that environmental protection had to come from the grass roots, not from a government that still adhered to the Hoover philosophy. Indeed, some felt that the government and its agencies—in this case the Army Corps of Engineers—needed watching.

Finally, the accelerating costs of the Vietnam War collided with the mushrooming costs of the dam and national park. Something had to give.

But all this transpired over more than twenty years. The dam might still have been built while these opposing forces gained momentum had it not been for a handful of women and men who loved Sunfish Pond and the free-flowing Delaware River and its valley. Against huge odds they fought and finally won the battle for Tocks Island.

The next time you canoe through Walpack Bend or the Water Gap, or hike on the Appalachian Trail past Sunfish Pond, think of them.

18

SQUATTERS

The Army Corps of Engineers had a problem. They were expected to build a dam at Tocks Island, as well as a recreation area around it, with ever-shrinking funds—funds that some members of Congress wanted to use to fight the war in Vietnam. One source of additional cash might be the rental of vacant homes in the dam area, purchased by the corps from unhappy owners. These homes would be destroyed when dam construction began, but in the meantime the rent would help the money situation and also prevent the vandalism and arson then rampant.

Sometime in mid-1969, then, the corps ran "House for Rent" ads in the New York City papers—including, oddly enough, that champion of hippiedom, the *Village Voice*. Almost immediately, Interstate 80 took on a *Grapes of Wrath* ambience with old cars, motorcycles, and hikers with blanket rolls, all heading west. Communes and "families" were soon established in the dam area, especially on the Jersey side of the river. These flower children, intent on creating a self-sufficient farming society based on love and togetherness, settled first in an encampment that they called Cloud Farm. Others followed and, with or without leases, soon occupied all of the vacant buildings on the Jersey side. The overflow crossed to Pennsylvania and moved into vacated houses there. These new residents referred to themselves as river people; everyone else called them squatters.

By 1970 the Corps had second thoughts about the advantages of landlordship and did not renew the leases on the Cloud Farm and other hippie enclaves in New Jersey. Some of the river people refused to leave voluntarily and a force of armed Jersey troopers removed them. Many of the evictees moved in with their friends on the Pennsylvania side of the river.

In the Keystone State the squatters settled in an area of the reservoir and park site called the Minisink, just above Shawnee-on-Delaware. The first arrivals, such as New Yorkers Bill Read and family and Dorothy Belmont and her husband, seemed conventional enough. But some that followed were much less so. Richard Albert, in his book *Damming the Delaware,* describes the scene: "Scattered among the houses were tent camps, Indian teepees, homemade structures, and a variety of innovative hippie homes including one geodesic dome built on a raft in the Delaware." Some moved into an abandoned church and grew marijuana in its cemetery.

Soon, the hippie presence was noticed in nearby villages, especially in Stroudsburg and East Stroudsburg. There the longhaired, barefoot, not-always-clean interlopers were looked on with distaste. They were, after all, living free in the homes that hardworking, longtime residents had been forced out of. Distaste turned to anger when several of the squatters applied for and received welfare. When authorities asked them to work for the hand-out, they refused due to lack of transportation. The local citizenry paid for this welfare with their municipal taxes—and resented it profoundly.

The *Pocono Record* began receiving letters to the editor that expressed this feeling. "P. E." from Saylorsburg wrote: "They want to live in homes that people worked all their lives to pay for. . . . They want us to support them. . . . They are trash and we would be better off if they left our beautiful Poconos. . . . Do away with their welfare. It may help if they go hungry." Apparently, authorities didn't follow this advice. The *Record* reported in November 1972 that fifty-nine of the river people in Monroe County were receiving welfare. The paper hinted, too, that some of these might be double-dipping in New Jersey.

Some critics did more than write letters. A favorite Saturday night's entertainment for some young men was a drive through the Minisink to shoot out windows, kill pets and farm animals, shout obscenities, and, it was said, burn a barn or two (this last act invariably blamed on the hippies). Two river people were wounded in drive-by shootings. When a man who had been fishing drowned in the river, hippies were accused of causing his death, although no charges were ever filed. Dedicated to nonviolence, the hippies in 1971 petitioned Monroe County for police protection. Before the police could act, though, the Army Corps of Engineers moved in to "deal with the unhealthy problems that exist in the area of . . . vandalism and dope."

At 6 A.M. on Friday, September 3, 1971, teams of shotgun-toting federal marshals accompanied two bulldozers in an attack on twenty hippie-occupied houses in the Minisink. The force blitzed six houses and a pup tent before the flower children took action. Banko Omedelli, leader of the Squatters' Parents Committee, climbed up a tree and thence to the roof of his threatened home, where his rash defiance cowed the dozer operator. Uwe Dramm, a twenty-one-year-old former missionary, did the same, accompanied by his wife, two children, and assorted cats. Several others simply stood before their houses or barns and blocked the approaching machines. The task force pulled back for consultation with the corps' officer in charge, and this colonel declared a cease-fire. Omedelli, a writer of children's books, sent telegrams to the president, Governor Milton Shapp of Pennsylvania, and the secretary of the army. He said, "I think that when an armed force moves in on a helpless and non-violent people, the United States should come to our help." The squatters bought time—but not acceptance.

Thus began a long court battle between the squatters and the Army Corps of Engineers. The Justice Department in 1972 filed suit to evict the river people, which now numbered 171, and stated that their "continued occupancy within Tocks has resulted . . . in irreparable damage to the United States." Squatters' appeals in the distict court in Scranton kept delaying the evictions. The squatters held that the reservoir and national park site were public lands, and that they themselves were the public. Officials of the State of Pennsylvania remained strangely silent through it all.

Local anger and fear grew. In 1972 the *Pocono Record* fanned emotions with a series of articles titled "Crisis Along the Delaware." The first article stated that "federal officials fear an outbreak of armed conflict" and described the squatter encampment as a way station for fugitives from justice on their way to Canada or Mexico, as well as a major drug distribution center. *Record* reporters wrote that the operation was so efficient that the fugitives "cannot be traced by the F.B.I."

Subsequent articles spoke of the large number of arsons in the area, but admitted that the fires might have been set by native residents trying to keep additional squatters from moving in. When rangers built a snowmobile trail, reporters wrote, a wire was stretched across the trail "at neck level," presumably by squatters. Squatter morals, or lack of them, was another sore point. The *Record* described nude squatters "cavorting obnoxiously" by the river and told of some who "do more without their clothes than just swim." One free-spirited woman, they said, shopped repeatedly at the Shawnee General Store—in the nude.

In November 1972 federal marshals and Pennsylvania State police again entered the Minisink, this time to serve notice of legal proceedings aimed at eviction. Things went calmly enough until a hippie attempted to escape the scene on his bicycle and had to be wrestled to the ground by two state troopers and a marshal. When a crowd gathered, extra troopers were called in and the runaway biker was hauled off to jail. The notices served, the government forces left amid catcalls and jibes. One prescient hippie shouted after them, "We'll see you again next year."

Appeals by the squatters' lawyers, working on the cuff, postponed any action for many months. In June 1973 Army Corps of Engineers officials reported that the hippies were stockpiling arms and building bunkers. They predicted armed resistance, another Wounded Knee massacre. Hippies denied collecting weapons and said the bunkers were simply additional buildings for newcomers to inhabit. Even the *Pocono Record* accused the corps of "overstating" the situation. The appeal process continued into February 1974, when federal judge Michael Sheridan, sitting in Wilkes-Barre, denied the squatters' final plea.

On Monday, February 25, a paramilitary force of ninety federal marshals met at the Honeymoon Hideaway in Dingmans Ferry—a scene of far happier assignations—and planned for the attack. They targeted sixty-five squatters living along a three-mile stretch of riverside near Shawnee. The marshals had shotguns and tear gas canisters, in addition to their usual sidearms, and each received a bullet-proof vest to wear under his blue jumpsuit. Early on Wednesday morning, with the temperature thirteen degrees, this force and dozens of state troopers moved into the Minisink. The troopers stayed on the perimeter and blocked off the roads; no outsiders, including members of the press, were allowed in until the operation was concluded.

The force did not achieve complete surprise though. Barry Kohn, head of the state's Civil Tension Task Force, had attempted to alert the squatters by telephone the night before without luck—there were no phone or electric lines into the area—then drove to the Minisink. He warned the squatters of the imminent raid, but the river people did nothing; they believed their appeal was still pending. Had the squatters planned armed resistance as the Army Corps of Engineers predicted, Kohn's action could have led to disaster.

The river people were taken from their homes with no chance to collect possessions, then marched down River Road to checkpoints outside the federal area. At the checkpoints they were left to their own devices, but they could not return to the Minisink. In addition to abandoning personal property and pets, the squatters left behind a variety of farm animals and old cars. Marshals collected a few weapons—mostly hunting rifles, axes, and bows and arrows—and a small amount of dope. Of the group being evicted, several were children (including newborn babies). One father, Ralph Rosario, carried a daughter he had helped deliver just ten hours earlier; the new mother walked unsteadily beside him. A few mothers on public assistance, and their children, were permitted to spend that night in the local welfare office. When the press chided the Justice Department for its treatment of the pregnant women, a department representative said this could not be a consideration, since "if [the mothers] worked it right they could have a baby every day or so."

The hippies offered little resistance to the raid. Many of them collected at the roadblocks, singing songs and dancing to guitar music. But eleven men and women refused to leave and were handcuffed, kept in a van for a few hours, then taken outside the area and released. Banko Omedelli was among them and after his release he worked to locate money, shelter, and transportation for his people. Some of the evictees were taken in by local residents, who, although they weren't crazy about hippies, hated the Army Corps of Engineers— and their dam—even more.

The larger domestic animals were a problem. The squatters had left behind twenty horses, twelve cows, a mule, and an assortment of turkeys, chickens, ducks, pigs, and goats. Ed Cantrill, manager of the local SPCA, had not been told in advance about the raid and now was overwhelmed. These animals had to be fed and sheltered and the cows needed to be milked. When Cantrill suggested to the marshals that small groups of squatters be allowed to claim their livestock, the marshals refused. Cantrill got the job done anyway.

Demolition crews, which had been held in waiting, went into action as soon as the area was cleared of people. They pushed over or burned some stone houses and reduced the frame houses and barns to kindling. Most of the squatters' personal possessions and many of the pets were lost in this operation. In its zeal to deny shelter to any future invaders, the corps knocked down many historic structures and gutted the church that the hippies had lived in and cared for. A restraining order finally had to be issued to stop this senseless destruction.

The press, angry at being kept away from the eviction, attacked the corps with a vengeance. The treatment of the hippies and the wanton destruction of historic homes along the river added fuel to the fire. Newspaper editorials and broadsides turned ever more people against the corps and against the Tocks Island project as a whole. Public support for the dam, already eroding, virtually disappeared. In this war for the Delaware Valley, the most formidable enemy the Army Corps of Engineers faced was . . . itself.

19

THE
BIG
ICE

he path of the Delaware River through the Mini-sink is a troubled one indeed; its flow seems to have been designed by some supernatural but deranged plumber. Wide and demure when it passes between Port Jervis and Matamoras, it goes berserk just below their connecting bridge. In the space of a mile or two it makes a perfect ninety degree turn from due east to due south, accepts the sometimes considerable inflow of the Neversink River, and then charges headlong between narrowed banks toward two substantial islands, Mashipacong and Thirsty Deer.

This configuration is harmless enough when water levels are normal or nearly so but it can result in the flooding of bottomland during periods of heavy rainfall or snowmelt. And it causes absolute disaster when rising winter waters carrying monster chunks of ice push into the island bottleneck, plugging the valley like a giant cork. With this ice dam in place, the river overflows in a flash and backs up into the two cities. The thick, frozen slabs can crush houses, bridges,

and cars and level whole business districts without the slightest de-
terrence. Such ice gorges, peculiar to this area of the river, happen periodically, and their devastation increases with the growth in
population.

These destructive ice floods have been described in journals and
newspapers since colonial times. Washington, when he crossed the
river at Trenton on that fateful Christmas night, dealt with major ice
in the river—an upriver gorge on its way to the sea. So bad was the
ice that two arms of his pincer movement—two-thirds of his force—
couldn't get across. The Bridges Freshet of January 1841 received its
name when ice wiped out nearly all the spans crossing the river. As
populations grew and the number of both pedestrian and railroad
bridges increased, ice gorges became more infamous.

In 1875 an ice jam threatened the upper valley for most of February and March; low water levels, ironically, caused the full depth of
the river to freeze solid. When the rains came they raised up the huge
slabs, piled one atop the other, and moved them slowly but inex-
orably downriver. Occasionally, this ice gorge would jam the river at
a narrow spot, flood villages and farms, then break free under the
mounting water pressure and start moving again.

Throughout February and into early March this monster inched
along. The good citizens of Port Jervis and Matamoras, kept aware of
the approaching menace by railroad telegraphers on the route, waited
helplessly. As it drew near, the ice dam picked up an iron railroad
bridge, Delaware Number Two, and carried it intact atop the piled-
up ice. When this juggernaut reached the wooden Barrett Bridge
between the two cities, it sliced through without a pause; now two
bridges straddled the floe. On March 17, Saint Patricks Day, the
whole thing stopped dead at the bottleneck at Mashipacong Island.

The people of Port Jervis and Matamoras headed for the high
ground, with or without their worldly possessions, as huge ice slabs
scoured through flooded neighborhoods on either bank. As the water pressure built, the Erie Railroad management tried to protect its
property by exploding a huge charge of nitroglycerine set in the dam.

The blast shook the whole tri-state area, but it broke things loose. The ice clot moved on, dropping its captive bridges along the way. Commercial activity in Port Jervis and Matamoras slowed considerably, and the two cities were cut off from each other for more than a month. That summer, farmers marveled at the giant ice slabs in their pastures, and Fourth-of-July libations were cooled by remnants of the ice gorge.

In March 1904 a gorge formed due to a long, frozen winter followed by heavy rains. The *Port Jervis Evening Gazette* headlines called it the "Worst Gorge Ever Known" and described the episode as a "Night of Terror in Port Jervis." The terror was caused by tidal waves that surged through the lower parts of both Port Jervis and Matamoras. As water pressure built behind the ice dam, the blockage would break free, then plug up again, then break free again, all the while causing new waves. Sometimes, flood watchers were caught in a wave and sent running for their lives; several barely escaped in the shoulder-deep ice water. Bridge damage remained minimal because most pedestrian spans had been swept away in the Pumpkin Freshet of the previous October and had not yet been replaced. The railroad bridge between Matamoras and Port Jervis, high above the waters of the October flood, fell victim to the river's piled-up ice slabs; the whole thing toppled over on its side and disappeared. As soon as the ice dam broke, the water level dropped to normal and the cities dried out.

Each generation claims its own ice gorge to be the worst. The most recent one, as of this writing, arrived in the tri-state area on Valentine's Day in 1981. The U.S. Geological Survey stream gauge at Port Jervis for that February 12 showed a flood stage of 26.6 feet— the highest ever recorded on the gauge, and a full foot higher than the previous record set during the ice flood of 1904. (The hurricane-induced rains that caused the deadly flood of 1955 fell downriver from the gauge and weren't recorded.)

The weather pattern preceding the Valentine's Day gorge was typical: a dry fall resulting in low water levels, followed by extremely

The ice-jammed Delaware at Port Jervis, New York, February 1981. (Photo courtesy of the Minisink Valley Historical Society, Port Jervis, New York)

cold temperatures that froze the river solid. When a heavy downpour fell that the frozen ground could not absorb, the rainwater rushed into the river and the ice floe started on its way. Again, the downriver glacier stopped dead in the narrows at Mashipacong Island. The river rose fourteen and a half feet in the first hour, then lowered, then raised again, this fluctuation caused by smaller upriver ice gorges breaking loose. The erratic behavior fooled everybody. In the two rivers bordering Port Jervis, the Delaware and the Neversink, observers noted huge ice cakes float downstream, reverse direction and go upstream, then reverse direction again. The *New York Times* wrote of John Lantini, who drove down First Street to the Delaware dike at four in the morning on the twelfth and found the river about to crest.

"I jumped into my car and drove down the street, honking my horn and yelling for everybody to get out," he said. "I parked the car, ran back to the house, and me and the wife grabbed what clothes we could. We were in water up to our knees when we got back out on the street."

One man living on Hammond Street, blocks from the river, took a 5 A.M. walk toward the dike. When he reached the Conrail overpass, he found water pouring through it. "I ran home as fast as I could . . . with the water chasing me," he said. Like many others, he didn't sleep at home that night.

People living in other riverside neighborhoods had similar experiences. Rescue squad personnel, police, and firefighters were busy on Front Street, Pike Street, Jersey Avenue, Ball Street, and King Street saving lives in sub-freezing temperatures and high winds. Some refugees left home so quickly they were barefoot; many of these would suffer frostbite. On Seward Avenue, twenty-one-year-old Charles Houghtaling carried an elderly neighbor, who showed signs of a heart attack, four blocks through waist-deep water and floating ice to an ambulance.

On the other side of town, the overflowing Neversink flooded Doctor's Sunnyside Hospital, and all patients were evacuated to nearby St. Francis Hospital.

Port Jervis's mayor, Arthur Gray, had schools and other public buildings accept evacuees, then arranged for meals. Before the day was over three thousand people from Port Jervis, Matamoras, and adjacent areas would be homeless.

For a while Port Jervis was isolated from Matamoras when the two river bridges closed. Ice ruptured a gas line on the Matamoras–Port Jervis bridge and the gas ignited. The fire spread to shore but did little damage, even though the shut-off valve for the gas line lay underwater and couldn't be closed until the water subsided. Ice also knocked down the steel tower carrying the trunk phone line over the river, and most communication subsequently had to be done by ham radio. Electric panel boards short-circuited in flooded basements and caused power outages and lack of heat in many homes. Plummeting temperatures compounded the discomfort. Fortunately, no lives were lost in Port Jervis.

A trailer park was hit hard in nearby Montague, New Jersey, on the shore of the usually placid Neversink. The *Union-Gazette* told of a retired couple who had moved in with a new deluxe mobile home the month before. Their unit was flooded to a depth of five feet, and huge ice cakes snapped off large trees nearby and crushed their home. The couple escaped with their lives but lost everything else. They had no insurance.

Popular Flo-Jean's Restaurant, perched attractively on the bank of the river, was badly damaged. This former toll house lost its large collection of historical weapons and other artifacts when the ice caved in a riverside wall. The flood also washed a truck into the dining room.

Matamoras also was hit hard. This city, built on the flats along the west bank of the river, floods more readily than Port Jervis in spite of some dikes. A log kept at the command center in Matamoras reveals the erratic behavior of the river in the early morning hours. Doug Hay and Nancy Barletto, in their reprise of the event, *The Ice Gorge Flood,* reproduced the log:

> 12:45 A.M. Ice jamming below Tri-States began to raise the river level.
> 1:25 A.M. River level was reported going down.
> 2:15 A.M. The river was reported rising . . .
> 2:40 A.M. Milford Bridge called, ice there on the move, gauge has dropped 20 points in 20 minutes.
> 3:25 A.M. River coming across the road . . .
> 3:30 A.M. River dropped three feet.
> 3:40 A.M. "All Hell Broke Loose!"

More than half of the residential area of Matamoras and its little suburb, Westfall, lay underwater. The Matamoras firehouse was cut off by the tidal wave, as was the Westfall control center a half mile inland. But the real damage was done by the huge chunks of ice, which

*The backyards of Port Jervis, New York, after the "big ice" of Valentine's Day 1981.
(Photo courtesy of the Minisink Valley Historical Society, Port Jervis, New York)*

smashed houses, wiped out foundations, tore off decks and porches, and carried away garages.

On Pennsylvania Avenue, the main thoroughfare, three moving cars were caught in the initial onrush of water and swept into a nearby field. The occupants had to climb on their cars' roofs to survive. Firefighters finally reached them by boat. Fire Chief Joseph Balch and firefighter Kevin Degroat rescued a woman on Pennsylvania Avenue who was neck deep in water. Sixty-five-year-old Rose Devins wasn't so lucky; she was apparently walking to a shelter when the floodwater overtook her. Her body was found that afternoon, amid chunks of ice, a half mile away. On Mashipacong Island, most people were rescued except for two stubborn couples who refused to leave but survived anyhow.

More than four hundred homes in Matamoras and Westfall were damaged, and most were not covered by flood insurance. Joseph Ricciardi, mayor of Matamoras, confirmed that the town was in worse shape now than after the 1955 calamity. "The '55 flood was in August so we didn't have to worry about the ice," he said.

At mid-morning the water disappeared as the gorge became unplugged. But reminders lay all over the place; huge chunks of ice remained on lawns, streets, and playgrounds, like the carcasses of beached whales.

Almost immediately the cleanup began. Fire companies from dozens of communities arrived to help, using pumps to get the water out of basements. Towns from as far away as Middletown and Warwick in New York, Newton and Hopatcong in New Jersey, and Stroudsburg and Hawley in Pennsylvania didn't wait to be asked. Even local fire and rescue companies went where help was needed most, without regard for boundaries; Matamoras pumps helped clean out Port Jervis basements and Port Jervis rescue squads saved people stranded in Matamoras. County and state crews soon arrived to help with the cleanup and national park rangers and Fish and Game commission personnel kept curiosity seekers and looters out of the area. Federal assistance began to trickle in, though not enough.

Tocks Island Dam advocates were now able to say, "I told you so," since the project would have put additional dikes along the riverfront. Those who wondered why the ice jam wasn't blasted as earlier ones had been were told that dynamite wouldn't have dented miles of ice. The Army Corps of Engineers recommended an ice escape chute be built at Mashipacong Island by clearing trees and constructing a two-hundred-foot path along the island's back channel. At this writing the ice-chute project on Mashipacong has been approved but the work hasn't yet been completed. Those tough islanders don't want to move.

Ironically, the day after the ice gorge calamity, a column appeared in the *Port Jervis Union Gazette* titled "Thoughts of Special Valentine's Day Linger." Obviously written before the flood, it talked a little about exchanging cards and gifts, but mostly it talked about caring for one another. In times of crisis the good people of the Delaware Valley have always done that.

INTRODUCTION

BOOKS

Cross, Dorothy. *The Indians of New Jersey.* Trenton, N.J.: Archaeological Society of New Jersey, 1958.

Grumet, Robert S. *The Lenape.* New York: Chelsea House Publishers, 1989.

Kraft, Herbert C. *The Lenape.* Newark, N.J.: New Jersey Historical Society, 1986.

————. *The Indians of Lenapehoking.* South Orange, N.J.: Seton Hall University Museum, 1985.

Price, Lynda. *Lenni-Lenape: New Jersey's Native People.* Paterson, N.J: Paterson Museum, 1980.

Thompson, Ray. *The Walking Purchase Hoax of 1737.* Fort Washington, Pa.: Bicentennial Press, 1973.

ARTICLES

"From Lenape Territory to Royal Province, 1600–1750." New Jersey State Museum, 1971.

Kraft, Herbert C., ed. "The Lenape Indian." A symposium at Seton Hall University, 1984.

"The Walking Purchase." Historical Pennsylvania Leaflet #24. Pennsylvania Historical and Museum Commission, Harrisburg, 1972.

1. Nasty Little Village

BOOKS

Chitwood, Oliver P. *A History of Colonial America.* New York: Harper Brothers, 1931.

Churchill, Winston. *A History of the English-Speaking People.* Vol. 2. New York: Dodd, Mead, & Company, 1956.

Federal Writers' Project of the Works Progress Administration for the State of Delaware. *Delaware—A Guide to the First State.* New York: Viking Press, 1938.

Garber, John P. *The Valley of the Delaware.* Port Washington, N.Y.: Ira Friedman, 1934.

Hine, C. G. *The Old Mine Road.* New Brunswick, N.J.: Rutgers University Press, 1963.

Jameson, J. F., ed. *Narratives of New Netherland 1609–1664.* New York: Barnes & Noble, 1909.

———, ed. *Narratives of Early American History 1630–1701.* New York: Barnes & Noble, 1907.

Lankford, John, ed. *Captain John Smith's America.* New York: Harper & Row, 1967.

Scharf, J. Thomas. *History of Delaware.* Philadelphia: L. J. Richards Company, 1888.

Weslager, Clinton A. *The English on the Delaware.* New Brunswick, N. J.: Rutgers University Press, 1967.

ARTICLES

"The Fin Whale." *New Jersey Outdoors,* Summer 1994.

2. LORD EDMUND PLOWDEN — ROYAL LOSER

BOOKS

Chitwood, Oliver P. *A History of Colonial America.* New York: Harper Brothers, 1931.

Churchill, Winston. *A History of the English-Speaking People.* Vol. 2. New York: Dodd, Mead, & Company, 1956.

Garber, John P. *The Valley of the Delaware.* Port Washington, N.Y.: Ira Friedman, 1934.

Jameson, J. F., ed. *Narratives of New Netherland 1609–1664.* New York: Barnes & Noble, 1909.

———, ed. *Narratives of Early American History 1630–1701.* New York: Barnes & Noble, 1907.

Lankford, John, ed. *Captain John Smith's America.* New York: Harper & Row, 1967.

Pennington, John. *Pennsylvania Historical Society Memoirs.* Vol. 4. Philadelphia: McCarty & Dari, 1840.

Weslager, Clinton A. *The English on the Delaware 1610–1682.* New Brunswick, N. J.: Rutgers University Press, 1967.

Wildes, Harry Emerson. *The Delaware.* New York: Farrar Company, 1940.

3. TIMBER RAFTS ON THE RIVER

BOOKS

Banks, Ivy Jackson. *Banks of the Delaware.* Trenton, N.J.: Trenton Historical Society, 1967.

Cummins, George. *History of Warren County.* New York: Lewis Historical Publishing Company, 1911.

Curtis, Charles T. *Rafting on the Delaware.* Ithaca, N.Y.: Dewitt Historical Society of Tompkins County, 1957.

Hazard, Samuel. *Hazard's Register of Pennsylvania.* Philadelphia: W. F. Geddes Company, 1835.

Heller, William J. *Historic Easton.* Easton, Pa.: Express Publishing Company, 1911.

Henry, Ruth. *The Portland Press.* Unpublished, manuscript on deposit at Easton Public Library, 1955.

Hoff, Wallace. *Two Hundred Miles on the Delaware River.* Trenton, N.J.: Brandt Press, 1893.

Johnston, John Willard. *Reminiscences.* Highland, N.Y.: The Reporter Company, 1987.

Lee, Warren F. *Down along the Old Bel-Del.* Easton, Pa.: Bel-Del Enterprises, 1987.

Letcher, Gary. *Canoeing the Delaware River.* New Brunswick, N.J.: Rutgers University Press, 1985.

McIlhaney, Asa K. *Historical Notes.* Unpublished manuscript at Easton Public Library, 1956.

Pine, Joshua. *Rafting Story of the Delaware.* Unpublished manuscript on deposit at Easton Public Library, 1883.

Schrabisch, Max. *Archaeology of the Delaware River Valley.* Trenton, N.J.: MacCrellish & Quigley, 1917.

Snell, James P. *History of Sussex and Warren Counties.* Philadelphia: Everts & Peck, 1881.

Stutz, Bruce. *Natural Lives, Modern Times.* New York: Crown Publishers, 1992.

Weiss, Harry and Grace. *Rafting on the Delaware River.* Trenton, N.J.: New Jersey Agricultural Society, 1967.

Wildes, Harry Emerson. *The Delaware.* New York: Farrar Company, 1940.

Wood, Leslie. *Rafting on the Delaware River.* Livingston Manor, N.Y.: Livingston Manor Times, 1934.

ARTICLES

"Rafting on the Delaware." *Two Hundred Years of Life in Northampton County.* Northampton County Bicentennial Commission, 1976.

"Rafts of the Delaware." *Historical Articles of the Delaware Valley.* Warren County Daughters of the American Revolution, Hackettstown Historical Society, 1939.

Curtis, Mary E. "Songs and Stories of the Raftsmen." Unpublished manuscript at Minisink Historical Society, Port Jervis, N.Y.

NEWSPAPERS

Easton Daily Argus. July 5, 1876.
Hunterdon Democrat. February 9, 1870.
Port Jervis Daily Union. April 20, 1880.
Port Jervis Evening Gazette. April 29, 1869.
Port Jervis Evening Gazette. April 9, 1870.

MISCELLANEOUS

Smith, Christine. Taped interview in Mount Bethel, Pa., August 18, 1990.
"Upper Delaware." Brochure with map issued by National Park Service,
    GPO 1986, 491-417/40946, Department of the Interior.

4. MR. DURHAM'S BOAT

BOOKS

Alderfer, E. Gordon. *Northampton Heritage.* Easton, Pa.: Northampton County
    Historical and Genealogical Society, 1953.
Anderson, John A. *Navigating on the Upper Delaware.* Trenton, N.J.: MacCrell-
    ish & Quigley, 1913.
Banks, Ivy Jackson. *Banks of the Delaware.* Trenton, N.J.: Trenton Historical
    Society, 1967.
Brodhead, Luke. *The Delaware Water Gap.* Philadelphia: Sherman Company,
    1870.
Chastellux, Marquis de. *Travels in North America.* Chapel Hill: University of
    North Carolina Press, 1963.
Coggins, Jack. *Ships and Seamen of the American Revolution.* Harrisburg, Pa.:
    Stackpole Books, 1969.
Cohen, David S. *Folklife in New Jersey.* Trenton, N.J.: New Jersey Historical
    Commission, 1982.
Commager, Henry Steele, and Richard B. Morris, eds., *The Spirit of 'Seventy-
    Six.* New York: Bonanza Books, 1983.
Cummins, George. *History of Warren County.* New York: Lewis Historical
    Publishing Company, 1911.

Fast, Howard. *The Crossing.* New York: Morrow Company, 1971.

Heller, William J. *Historic Easton.* Easton, Pa.: Express Publishing Company, 1911.

Lebegern, George F. *Episodes in Bucks County History.* Doylestown, Pa.: Bucks County Historical and Tourist Commission, 1975.

Letcher, Gary. *Canoeing the Delaware River.* New Brunswick, N.J.: Rutgers University Press, 1985.

Pohl, John Charles. *Local Sketches and Legends of Early Easton.* Unpublished manuscript in Easton Public Library, 1949.

Richards, Jay C. *Penn, Patriots and the Pequest.* Belvidere, N.J.: Great Northern Commerical Services, 1995.

Smith, S. Stelle. *The Battle of Trenton.* Monmouth Beach, N.J.: Philip Freneau Press, 1965.

Wacker, Peter. *The Musconetcong Valley of New Jersey.* New Brunswick, N.J.: Rutgers University Press, 1968.

Wallace, Paul A. *Pennsylvania—Seed of a Nation.* New York: Harper & Row, 1962.

Wildes, Harry Emerson. *The Delaware.* New York: Farrar Company, 1940.

ARTICLES

"Ancient Commerce on the Delaware River." *Historical Articles of the Delaware Valley.* Warren County Daughters of the American Revolution, Hackettstown Historical Society, 1939.

"Durham Boats." *Two Hundred Years of Life in Northampton County.* Northampton County Bicentennial Commission, 1976.

Fackenthal, Benjamin Franklin. "Improving Navigation on the Delaware River." A paper read at the Bucks County Historical Society, September 10, 1927. Published in *Bucks County Historical Society Papers,* 1932.

———. "General Washington and His Army Crossing the Delaware." *Bucks County Historical Society Paper,* 1934.

"Philadelphia Fever." *American Heritage,* July/August 1993, pp. 98–99.

Skirbst, Henry. "Tales and Trails." *Hackettstown Gazette,* July 18, 1989.

"Victory at Trenton." *New Jersey Outdoors,* November/December 1988.

"Washington Crossing the Delaware." Pamphlet produced by the Washington Crossing Foundation, Washington Crossing, Pa., 1990.

TAPED INTERVIEW

Hicks, Homer. Belvidere, N.J., August 21, 1990.

5. THE RIVER IN WAR

BOOKS

Chastellux, Marquis de. *Travels in North America.* Chapel Hill: University of North Carolina Press, 1963.

Coggins, Jack. *Ships and Seamen of the American Revolution.* Harrisburg, Pa.: Stackpole Books, 1969.

Commager, Henry Steele, and Richard B. Morris, eds. *The Spirit of 'Seventy-Six.* New York: Bonanza Books, 1983.

Fast, Howard. *The Crossing.* New York: Morrow Company, 1971.

Higgenbotham, Don. *The War of American Independence.* New York: Macmillan Company, 1971.

Lender, Mark E. *The River.* Trenton, N.J.: New Jersey Historical Commission, 1977.

Martin, Joseph Plumb. *Private Yankee Doodle.* Reprint, Salem, N.H.: Ayer Publishing Company, 1985.

Smith, Page. *A New Age Now Begins.* Vol. 2. New York: McGraw-Hill Book Company, 1976.

Smith, S. Stelle. *Fight for the Delaware, 1777.* Monmouth Beach, N.J.: Philip Freneau Press, 1970.

Stryker, William. *The Forts on the Delaware in the Revolutionary War.* Trenton, N.J.: John L. Murphy Publishing Company, 1901.

6. MASSACRE AT MINISINK

BOOKS

Commager, Henry Steele, and Richard B. Morris, eds. *The Spirit of 'Seventy-Six.* New York: Bonanza Books, 1983.

Eckert, Allan W. *The Wilderness War.* Boston: Little, Brown, and Company, 1978.

Gelb, Norman. *Less Than Glory.* New York: G. P. Putnams, 1984.

Leslie, Vernon. *The Battle of Minisink.* Middletown, N.Y.: Emmett Henderson Publisher, 1975.

Richards, Mark V. *Sesquicentennial of the Battle of Minisink.* Monticello, N.Y.: Republican Watchman, 1929.

Smith, Page. *A New Age Now Begins.* Vol. 2, New York: McGraw-Hill Book Company, 1976.

Stickney, Charles E. *A History of the Minisink Region.* Middletown, N.Y.: Coe, Finch, and I. F. Guiwits Publishers, 1867.

Stone, William L. *Life of Joseph Brant-Thayendegea.* New York: Blake, 1838.

Wallace, Anthony. *The Death and Rebirth of the Seneca.* New York: Alfred A. Knopf, 1972.

Weslager, Clinton A. *The Delaware Indians.* New Brunswick, N.J.: Rutgers University Press, 1972.

Wright, Esmond, ed. *The Fire of Liberty.* New York: St. Martin's Press, 1983.

7. The First Steamboat

BOOKS

Brandt, Francis Burke. *The Majestic Delaware.* Philadelphia: Brandt & Gummere Company, 1929.

Flexner, James Thomas. *Steamboats Come True.* Boston: Little, Brown, & Company, 1978.

Garber, John Palmer. *The Valley of the Delaware.* Chicago: John C. Winston Company, 1934.

Prager, Frank D., ed. *The Autobiography of John Fitch.* Philadelphia: American Philosophical Society, 1929.

Snell, James P. *History of Sussex and Warren Counties.* Philadelphia: Everts & Peck, 1881.

Federal Writers' Project of the Works Progress Administration for the State of New Jersey. *Stories of New Jersey.* New York: Hastings House, 1939.

8. STANDOFF AT LACKAWACK

BOOKS

Curtis, Charles T. *Rafting on the Delaware.* Ithaca, N.Y.: Dewitt Historical Society of Tompkins County, 1957.

Curtis, Mary. *Songs and Stories of the Raftsmen.* Unpublished manuscript at Minisink Historical Society, Port Jervis, N.Y.

Hazard, Samuel. *Hazard's Register of Pennsylvania.* Philadelphia: W. F. Geddes Company, 1835.

Jervis, John B. *Reminiscences.* Syracuse, N.Y.: Syracuse University Press, 1971.

Johnston, John Willard. *Reminiscences.* Highland, N.Y.: Reporter Company, 1987.

Lee, James. *Tales the Boatmen Told.* Easton, Pa.: Delaware Press, 1977.

LeRoy, Edwin D. *The Delaware and Hudson Canal—A History.* Honesdale, Pa.: Wayne County Historical Society, 1950.

McIlhaney, Asa K. *Historical Notes.* Unpublished manuscript at Easton Public Library, 1956.

Pine, Joshua. *Rafting Story of the Delaware.* Unpublished manuscript at Easton Public Library, 1883.

Sanderson, Dorothy H. *The Delaware and Hudson Canal Way.* Ellenville, N.Y.: Roundout Valley Publishing Company, 1965.

Shaughnessy, James. *Delaware and Hudson—Towpath to Tidewater.* Berkeley, Calif.: Howell-North Books, 1967.

Vogel, Robert M. *Roebling's Delaware and Hudson Canal Aqueducts.* Washington, D.C.: Smithsonian Institution, 1971.

Wakefield, Manville. *Coal Boats to Tidewater.* Grahamsville, N.Y.: Wakefair Press, 1965.

Weiss, Harry and Grace. *Rafting on the Delaware River.* Trenton, N.J.: New Jersey Agricultural Society, 1967.

Wood, Leslie. *Rafting on the Delaware River.* Livingston Manor, N.Y.: Livingston Manor Times, 1934.

NEWSPAPERS

Easton Daily Argus. April 18, 1829.
Middletown Daily Record. March 21, 1958.

Port Jervis Evening Gazette. March 19, 1870.
Port Jervis Evening Gazette. April 9, 1870.
Wayne County Herald. January 1, 1880.

9. GETTER'S ISLAND

BOOKS

Alderfer, E. Gordon. *Northampton Heritage.* Easton, Pa.: Northampton County Historical and Genealogical Society, 1953.
Minnich, Richard. *The Getter Murder.* Unpublished manuscript at Easton Public Library, 1949.
Pohl, John Charles. *Local Sketches and Legends of Early Easton.* Unpublished manuscript at Easton Public Library, 1949.

NEWSPAPERS

Easton Express. April 17, 1993.

10. THE LAST STEAMBOAT

BOOKS

Alderfer, E. Gordon. *Northampton Heritage.* Easton, Pa.: Northampton County Historical and Genealogical Society, 1953.
Brodhead, Luke. *The Delawre Water Gap.* Philadelphia: Sherman Company, 1870.
Cummins, George. *History of Warren County.* New York: Lewis Historical Publishing Company, 1911.
Lee, Warren F. *Down along the Old Bel-Del.* Easton, Pa.: Bel-Del Enterprises, 1987.
Pohl, John Charles. *Local Sketches and Legends of Early Easton.* Unpublished manuscript at Easton Public Library, 1949.

Snell, James P. *A History of Sussex and Warren Counties.* Philadelphia: Everts & Peck, 1881.

ARTICLES

"Alfred Thomas Explosion." *Two Hundred Years of Life in Northampton County.* Northampton County Bicentennial Commission, 1976.

NEWSPAPERS

New York Times. March 7, 1860.

11. THE PEA PATCH

BOOKS

Catton, Bruce. *Grant Moves South.* Boston: Little, Brown, and Company, 1960.
———. *Grant Takes Command.* Boston: Little, Brown, and Company, 1968.
Frank, William I., ed. *The Story of Fort Delaware.* Wilmington, Del.: Wilmington Printing Company.
Grant, U. S. *Personal Memoirs.* New York: Charles Webster Company, 1886.
Hamilton, A. J. *A Fort Delaware Journal.* Wilmington, Del.: Fort Delaware Society, 1981.
Handy, Isaak W. K. *United States Bonds.* Baltimore: Turnball Brothers, 1874.
Hesseltine, William. *Civil War Prisons.* Kent, Ohio: Kent State University Press, 1972.
Keen, Nancy T. *Confederate Prisoners of War at Fort Delaware.* Wilmington, Del.: Fort Delaware Society, 1968.
Parks, Robert. *Diary.* Southern Historical Society Papers.
Randall, J. G. *Lincoln the President.* New York: Dodd, Mead, & Company, 1952.
Shotwell, Randolph. *A Diary.* Raleigh, N.C.: 1931.
War of the Rebellion: A Compilation of the Official Records of the Union and Confederate Armies. 2nd ser., vol. 8. Washington, D.C.: 1899.

Wilson, W. E. *Delaware in the Civil War.* Dover, Del.: Civil War Centennial Commission, 1964.

————. *Fort Delaware.* Newark, Del.: University of Delaware Press, 1957.

————, *Fort Delaware in the Civil War.* Wilmington, Del.: Fort Delaware Society, 1964.

————, ed. *General M. Jeff Thompson in Fort Delaware.* Wilmington, Del.: Fort Delaware Society, 1972.

ARTICLES

Catton, Bruce. "Prison Camps of the Civil War." *American Heritage,* August 1959.

Fort Delaware Notes. Vol. 22, No. 1, January 1972; Vol. 28, April 1978; Vol. 30, April 1980; Vol. 44, February 1994.

Moon, W. H. "Prison Life at Fort Delaware." *Confederate Veteran.* Vol. 15, 1907.

Prison Times. Vol. 1, No. 1. April 1865.

12. MANUNKA CHUNK HOUSE

BOOKS

Cummins, George. *History of Warren County.* New York: Lewis Historical Publishing Company, 1911.

Lee, Warren F. *Down along the Old Bel-Del.* Easton, Pa.: Bel-Del Enterprises, 1987.

Snell, James P. *History of Warren and Sussex Counties.* Philadelphia: Everts & Peck, 1881.

Taber, Thomas, III. *The Delaware, Lackawanna and Western Railroad in the Twentieth Century.* Muncy, Pa.: Self-published, 1980.

ARTICLES

McGarrity, Margaret. "Looking Back at the Delaware Water Gap." *Warren County Magazine,* 1990.

NEWSPAPERS

Easton Express. October 16, 1903.
Easton Express. June 14, 1938.
Easton Express-Times. May 18, 1972.
New Jersey Herald. October 15, 1903
New York Times. October 10, 1903.
Sunday Call. February 11, 1934.

TAPED INTERVIEWS

Berger, Dale. New Jersey Division of Forests and Parks, March 9, 1993.
Dopke, William. Mount Bethel, Pa., April 1, 1993.
Lifer, William. Washington, N.J., March 9, 1993.
Ransom, Richard. Belvidere, N.J., April 7, 1993.
Smith, Mabel. Mount Bethel, Pa., March 7, 1993.

MISCELLANEOUS

"Beautiful Manunka Chunk Island Farm." Brochure. Ransom & Ruthinger.
Map of Manunka Chunk Island. State of New Jersey, Department of Parks
 and Recreation, Trenton, N.J.

13. The Pumpkin Freshet of 1903

BOOKS

Curtis, Charles T. *Rafting on the Delaware.* Ithaca, N.Y.: Dewitt Historical So-
 ciety of Tompkins County, 1957.
Dildine, Charles, and Homer Rasely. *Flood at Belvidere, New Jersey.* Belvidere:
 Privately published, 1903.
Shank, William. *Great Floods of Pennsylvania.* Privately published. Easton
 Public Library Historical Collection.

ARTICLES

Fackenthal, Benjamin Franklin. "Improving Navigation on the Delaware River." *Bucks County Historical Society Papers,* 1932.

NEWSPAPERS

Belvidere Apollo. October 16, 1903.
Belvidere Apollo. October 23, 1903.
Easton Express. October 10 – 13, 1903.
New Jersey Herald. October 15, 1903.
New York Times. October 6, 1903.
New York Times. October 10, 1903.
New York Times. October 27, 1903.

14. The Life and Times of Brainards

BOOKS

Cummins, George. *History of Warren County.* New York: Lewis Historical Publishing Company, 1911.
Lee, Warren F. *Down along the Old Bel-Del.* Easton, Pa.: Bel-Del Enterprises, 1987.
Shampanore, Frank. *History of Warren County.* Washington, N.J.: Frank Shampanore Press, 1929.

NEWSPAPERS

Easton Express. November 2, 1989.
Newton Sunday Herald. January 28, 1968.

TAPED INTERVIEWS

Barker, Pat. Hackettstown, N.J., October 1, 1992.
Chanda, Lillian. Phillipsburg, N.J., August 10, 1992.
Dorcsis, James. Brainards, N.J., September 18, 1992.
Dornich, John. Brainards, N.J., September 17, 1992.

15. THE GREAT CANOE MARATHON

BOOKS

Lee, Warren F. *Down along the Old Bel-Del.* Easton, Pa.: Bel-Del Enterprises, 1987.

NEWSPAPERS

Delaware Valley News. October 6, 1933.
Easton Express. October 10, 1933.
Easton Express. October 7, 1946.
Easton Express. October 12, 1946.
Hunterdon County Democrat. October 12, 1933.
Philadelphia Bulletin. October 8, 1933.
Philadelphia Inquirer. October 8, 1933.
Philadelphia Public Ledger. October 8, 1933.
Philadelphia Record. October 8, 1933.
Trenton State Gazette. October 6, 1933.

TAPED INTERVIEWS

Cooley, Howard. Frenchtown, N.J., October 9, 1990.
Hester, David. Wilson, Pa., July 30, 1992.
Hicks, Homer. Belvidere, N.J. December 4, 1990.
Norton, Rita Back. Easton, Pa., August 12, 1992.

Kleedorfer, Henry. Pen Argyl, Pa., June 14, 1992.
Kleedorfer, William. Mount Bethel, Pa., June 14, 1992.

MISCELLANEOUS

Hester, Clyde. Personal diary.
"First Annual Delaware Canoe Marathon." Official program.

16. THE BIG ONE OF '55

BOOKS

Diane Drowns the Delaware Valley. Easton: *Easton Express,* 1955.
Photo Highlights of Northeastern Pennsylvania's Worst Disaster. Carbondale: the
    Flood, 1955.
Shank, William. *Great Floods of Pennsylvania.* Manuscript in historical collec-
    tion at Easton Public Library.
The Flood of 1955. Reprinted from the *Blairstown Press.* Blairstown: 1955.

NEWSPAPERS

Easton Express. August 19 – 23, 1955.
Easton Express. October 5, 1955.
Newark Evening News. August 27, 1955.
New Jersey Herald. August 15 – 20, 1955.
New York Times. August 12 – 25, 1955.

TAPED INTERVIEWS

Baxter, Carl. Phillipsburg, N.J., September 22, 1993.
Brodt, Neil. Portland, Pa., August 29, 1990.
Brown, Len. Hackettstown, N.J., September 15, 1993.
Conrad, Betty. Wilson, Pa., October 22, 1990.
Harpster, Dick. Washington, N.J., September 5, 1990.

McNeillie, Marion. Branchville, N.J., June 23, 1992.
Steinman, Verne. Washington, N.J., September 9, 1990.
Wynkoop, Ron. Phillipsburg, N.J., September 12, 1990.

17. The Battle for Tocks Island

BOOKS

Albert, Richard C. *Damming the Delaware.* University Park: Pennsylvania State University Press, 1987.

Cary, John. *Historical Study of the Proposed Tocks Island Recreation Area.* Bethlehem, Pa.: Lehigh University.

Cummins, George. *History of Warren County.* New York: Lewis Historical Publishing Company, 1911.

Fulcomer, Kathleen. *The Delaware River.* New York: Seneca Press, 1981.

Horton, Robert. *A Program for Regulation and Conservation of the Delaware River.* Trenton, N.J.: Board of Commissioners, 1929.

Snell, James P. *History of Warren and Sussex Counties.* Philadelphia: Everts & Peck, 1881.

ARTICLES

Douglas, William O. "The Public Be Dammed." *Playboy Magazine.*

Lockwood, Harold A., Jr. "History of Public Policy Decisions Impacting the Delaware Water Gap Recreation Area: 1965 to the Present." Symposium on the twenty-fifth anniversary of the Delaware Water Gap Recreation Area, held at East Stroudsburg University, April 6–7, 1991.

NEWSPAPERS

Chicago Sun Times. April 24, 1972.
Chicago Sun Times. May 28, 1972.
Daily Record of Morris County. July 26, 1992.
Easton Express. August 20–22, 1955.

Easton Express-Times. July 19, 1992.
New York Times. August 20–25, 1955.
Phillipsburg Free Press. April 17, 1973.
Pocono Record. April 23, 1994.
Star Ledger (Newark, N.J.). July 15, 1992.

TAPED INTERVIEWS

Harpster, Richard. Washington, N.J., March 16, 1994.
Kays, Casey. Hackettstown, N.J., March 28, 1994.
Shukaitis, Nancy. East Stroudsburg, Pa., April 4, 1994.
Waldman, Mary. Blairstown, N.J., May 10, 1994.

MISCELLANEOUS

Carter, Jimmy. Statement on Sewell Bluff Dam, October 1, 1973.
Four-County Task Force on Tocks Island Dam. "Why the Four-County Task Force Is Opposed to Construction of the Tocks Island Dam." February 1972.
Hoover, Herbert. Speech made August 11, 1928.
Shukaitis, Nancy. Letter to author, April 25, 1994.
Shukaitis, Nancy. Statement before the American Society of Civil Engineers, Lehigh Valley Section, January 20, 1974.

18. SQUATTERS

BOOKS

Albert, Richard C. *Damming the Delaware.* University Park: Pennsylvania State University Press, 1987.

NEWSPAPERS

Easton Express-Times. July 19, 1992.
New Jersey Herald. February 27, 1974.

New York Times. February 27, 1971.
New York Times. September 7, 1971.
New York Times. February 18, 1974.
New York Times. February 28, 1974.
Pocono Record. November 18–28, 1972.
Pocono Record. June 14–21, 1973.
Pocono Record. February 17–28, 1974.

19. THE BIG ICE

BOOKS

Hay, Doug, and Nancy Barletto. *The Ice Gorge Flood.* Milford, Pa.: Pike County Dispatch, 1981.
U.S. Army Corps of Engineers. *Ice Related Flood Control Study.* Philadelphia: Custom House, 1986.

NEWSPAPERS

New York Times. February 12, 1981.
New York Times. February 13, 1981.
Port Jervis Evening Gazette. March 17, 1875.
Port Jervis Evening Gazette. March 9–17, 1904.
Port Jervis Evening Gazette. March 17, 1920.
Port Jervis Union-Gazette. February 5, 1981.
Port Jervis Union-Gazette. February 12–17, 1981.

INDEX

ABOUT THE AUTHOR

Frank Dale is a professional writer and regional historian. His articles have appeared in such publications as *Country Journal, New Jersey Outdoors, Skylander Magazine, Warren County Companion,* and *Pittsburgh Magazine.* Dale has won awards from the New Jersey Society of Professional Journalists, the Working Press Association, and the New Jersey Historical Commission. He and his wife currently live in Allamuchy, Warren County, New Jersey.